CW00338774

GREAT CENTRAL RAIL TOUR

The GREAT CENTRAL RAIL TOUR

JOHN M.C. HEALY

Dedication

To all those who worked on the Great Central, from its inception right up to its lamentable decline and eventual erasure from the British Railways network in 1966, and to the late S. W. A. Newton.

First published in 1988 by
UNICORN BOOKS
16 Laxton Gardens
Paddock Wood, Kent TN12 6BB

in conjunction with
SILVER STAR TRANSPORT BOOKS

Reprinted 1989

© John M. C. Healy

British Library Cataloguing in Publication Data
Healy, John M. C.
Great Central Rail tour.
1. England. Railway services: Great Central
Railway, to 1987–
I. Title
385'.0942

ISBN 1 85241 005 1

All rights reserved. No part of this publication may be reproduced, stored in a retrieval system, or transmitted in any form or by any means, electronic, mechanical, photocopying, recording or otherwise, without the prior permission of the publisher.

Typeset by Vitaset, Paddock Wood
Printed and bound by Biddles Ltd,
Guildford, Surrey

CONTENTS

ACKNOWLEDGEMENTS

I would like to thank the many people who have assisted in the preparation of this book, particularly the staff of the Leicestershire Record Office who have helped by putting their archive material at my disposal. I am also indebted to the *Leicester Mercury*, Real Photographs, Norman Steele, Hugh B. Oliver, David Bonas, Tom Boustead, Ken Fairey, Horace Gamble, M. King, John Hughes, W. L. Good, H. C. Casserley, Lens of Sutton and John Henton, who have all made their fine collections of photographs available to me. Their use has enabled me to study various aspects of the old Great Central London Extension Line and draw comparisons with scenes of the past and present side by side, representing the route during its construction, operation and sad passing into the annals of Railway Nostalgia. I am convinced that without the vivid recollections of former Great Central London Extension employees and photographers whom I have come across, it would not have been possible to create such an evocative book. This book would not be complete without mention of S. W. A. Newton and his pictorial record of the construction which serves as an inspiration to all followers of the Great Central.

PREFACE

The Manchester Sheffield and Lincoln Railway Company's London Extension, the dream of Sir Edward Watkin, had the distinction of being the last main line to reach the capital and its building was responsible for the evolution of the name Great Central, because the line cut a swathe straight down the central part of England through areas of scant population which gave it the reputation of a secondary route. Despite the line's importance as a freight-traffic carrier the London Extension has only managed to attract a considerable following and interest in it over the last twenty years, since it ceased to be a main-line railway and was eventually dismantled.

As far as the permanent way was concerned and the lineside buildings, the line more than proved itself to be one of the largest feats of Victorian engineering and, to aid such a task, the contractors were fortunate in having at their disposal a number of mechanical excavators and similar machinery which was in advance of its time. The construction of the route was carried out with speed and precision by a band of contractors working in seven sections. The future economy and efficiency of operation were the key notes of design as the line was to be subject to intense competition from the already existing railway companies. In this light, special attention was paid to fast running and all the usual obstacles such as level and farm crossings were bypassed with bridges or under-passes.

However, even these measures were to be of little help to the 'Central' as the railway which had so often teetered on the brink of collapse eventually fell victim to a decline in passenger and freight traffic, mainly brought about by the emergence of the motor car as a rival means of transport – the motor car/lorry having appeared at the beginning of the twentieth century, shortly after the opening of the London Extension. In the late 50s the line became labelled 'Duplicate', since some of the places it served were invariably catered for by its competitors. In fact it was this situation, coupled with the small stations generating an insufficient revenue, which led Dr Beeching, the famous Railway Axeman, to chop it up over a period of six years between 1960 and 1966 on the grounds that it was too costly to maintain.

Local stations ceased to operate in 1963, followed by the Main Line which was removed between Aylesbury and Rugby Central in 1966, leaving a rundown commuter service to linger on until 1969 when the last vestige of the London Extension was to disappear. However, at Loughborough Central soon after the end of all services, work began on the restoration of the station by the Main Line Preservation Group with a view to recreating part of the old Great Central, and by 1976 a new Great Central company was formed and the result enabled 5½ miles of track to be used by steam trains again.

Apart from this section and another seven miles retained for use by British Rail freight trains, all that remains is the skeleton of a once flourishing railway, along with some of the bridges, viaducts and tunnels that once reverberated with the passage of trains. This book is intended to conjure up some of the special atmosphere that was prevalent on the Great Central London Extension by giving a short description of the line's rise to fame and its subsequent demise. A series of photographic plates from the Newton collection is directly compared with the same scenes as they are today. As well as comparing the line's construction with its dereliction and return to nature, there is also a small section comparing the different motive power used by the various controlling bodies which operated the line, and one section comparing lineside views of trains with the same sites as they are today. Two parts of the book display the 'Then and Now' theme in a different fashion, with a portrait of Nottingham Victoria at the beginning . . . in its heyday . . . that is to be paralleled with its partner Marylebone which is covered towards the end of the volume. Because of the nature of present-day operations, the Loughborough to Rothley section is dealt with separately at the end of the book.

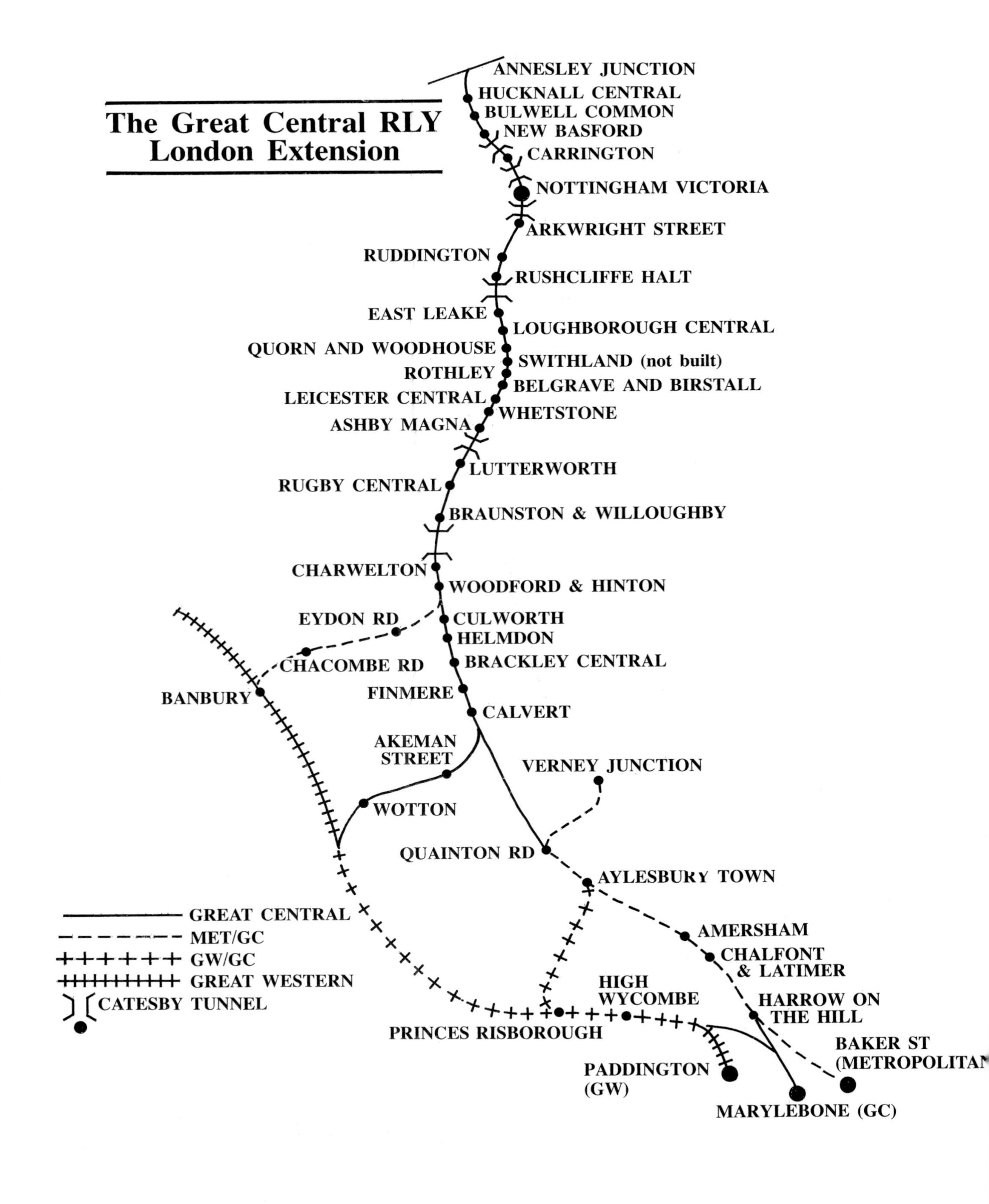

The Great Central RLY
London Extension
ANNESLEY JUNCTION
HUCKNALL CENTRAL
BULWELL COMMON
NEW BASFORD
CARRINGTON
NOTTINGHAM VICTORIA
ARKWRIGHT STREET
RUDDINGTON
RUSHCLIFFE HALT
EAST LEAKE
LOUGHBOROUGH CENTRAL
QUORN AND WOODHOUSE
SWITHLAND (not built)
ROTHLEY
BELGRAVE AND BIRSTALL
LEICESTER CENTRAL
WHETSTONE
ASHBY MAGNA
LUTTERWORTH
RUGBY CENTRAL
BRAUNSTON & WILLOUGHBY
CHARWELTON
WOODFORD & HINTON
EYDON RD
CULWORTH
HELMDON
CHACOMBE RD
BRACKLEY CENTRAL
BANBURY
FINMERE
CALVERT
AKEMAN STREET
VERNEY JUNCTION
WOTTON
QUAINTON RD
AYLESBURY TOWN
GREAT CENTRAL
MET/GC
GW/GC
GREAT WESTERN
CATESBY TUNNEL
AMERSHAM
CHALFONT & LATIMER
HIGH WYCOMBE
HARROW ON THE HILL
PRINCES RISBOROUGH
BAKER ST (METROPOLITAN
PADDINGTON (GW)
MARYLEBONE (GC)

SIR EDWARD WATKIN & HIS VISION

The Manchester Sheffield and Lincoln Railway Company's London Extension was the final main line to arrive in the capital. It formed part of the empire of a man called Edward Watkin, a wealthy Victorian entrepeneur, who was born in Ravald Street, Salford, Lancashire, in 1819, the son of a wealthy cotton merchant and highly-respected citizen, Absalom Watkin. Edward had two brothers, John and Alfred, who were also to become prominent figures. John became Vicar of Stoxwold in Lincolnshire while Alfred was Mayor of Manchester in 1873-4.

After a private education Edward Watkin entered his father's cotton business, though he soon moved on to other things as he got more and more interested in public affairs and, as director of the *Manchester Guardian*, he was a prominent figure in the arranging of literary soirees. As with other wealthy Victorians of the same social standing, Watkin involved himself in various enterprising schemes, namely raising money for the provision of amenities such as parks for the general public. In his capacity as secretary of the fund-raising committee he instigated the opening of three such parks in 1845. By this time Watkin's literary and business interests had increased his wealth and position and he went on to found the *Manchester Examiner* and to become a partner in his father's mill.

From the start of his rise to fame amongst his fellow Victorians it is clear to see that Watkin's ambition was to be the head of a vast empire. This began with him taking on the post of secretary of the Trent Valley Railway Company, which was later absorbed by the larger London North Western Railway for £438,000. Following this, he went on a short visit to the United States of America in 1851. An account of this visit was published two years later on his return to England, when he obtained his first major position as General Manager of the Manchester Sheffield and Lincolnshire Railway, which in later years was to be part of the longed-for empire.

Once firmly ensconced in his new position, Watkin entered into a series of negotiations with the Great Northern, Midland and North Western Railway Companies, in a bid to try and gain entry to London by obtaining running rights for his trains over other companies' tracks from the north and east. However the three companies concerned did not feel that they could entertain such competition and Watkin's plan failed.

In 1861 Watkin, at the wish of the Duke of Newcastle, travelled to Canada on Government business to investigate means by which the then five British states could be formed into a dominion. He had already considered the possibility of transferring the Hudson Bay Company to Government control, an expedient which was subsequently adopted in 1869. A further scheme was envisaged by him by which Quebec would be connected with the rest of the Canadian ports on the Atlantic coast.

Watkin returned from Canada and, after countless arguments with the directors of the Manchester, Sheffield and Lincoln Railway Company, he resigned his post as General Manager though in the next few years he obtained the following appointments:

1863 Co-directorship of the Manchester Sheffield and Lincoln (MS&L)
1864 (January)-1894 Chairman of the MS&L
1866 Directorship of the Great Western
1867 Directorship of the Great Eastern

In 1877 Watkin embarked on the initial stages of his dream to connect Liverpool and the Continent with the construction of the Liverpool and Manchester Railway, and by 1892 he had extended the Metropolitan Railway into the north of Buckinghamshire. Part of the network of this empire included the provision of a route between North and South Wales, incorporating a tunnel under the Mersey which allowed for a through rail connection to Lancashire. Watkin did not restrict his ambitious railway schemes to Britain but played an active part in construction of the line from Athens to Piraeus in Greece.

Watkin's first wife, Mary Briggs, whom he married in 1845, died at around this time (1887) and left a son, Alfred Mellor Watkin who, like the rest of the family, achieved notoriety and became MP for Grimsby. His sister, Harriet, married Worsley Taylor of Moreton Hall, Whaley. Watkin's second wife, Anne Little, lived only three years after their marriage and died in 1896, during the construction of the London Extension.

The building of the line that was soon to change the name of the railway from Manchester, Sheffield and Lincolnshire to Great Central was started in 1894. The intention was to extend the network from Beighton and Annesley in Sheffield to the Metropolitan in Buckinghamshire over which it would run to a point in London, where it could connect with the line to the coast at Dover. From there it would run under the Channel through a specially constructed tunnel to a French port and then to Paris. It took fifteen years for Watkin to succeed with his scheme, having first entered into a new set of negotiations when the Midlands and the Great Northern offered to lease the Manchester, Sheffield and Lincolnshire Railway or purchase it. The Midland backed out of negotiations but the Great Northern, who were Watkin's ally entered into a private deal, but even this was to come to nought because Watkin pitched his terms too high. Had this deal been accepted there would never have been a London Extension or a Great Central. Many people considered the construction of yet another railway into the capital was unnecessary since the Great Northern, Midland and other companies already provided an adequate service.

Watkin was left only one corridor in which to build the Great Central London Extension and this was the central part of England, an area which had not been filled because there were too many small villages to make a railway economically viable. Undeterred by this, Watkin went ahead with his plans to put these villages on the map and he hoped that maybe they would expand with the coming of the railway. Since the main criterion was economic and not social, cynics referred disparagingly to the Manchester, Sheffield and Lincolnshire as 'Money Sunk and Lost', and when it became Great Central it gained the nickname 'Gone Completely' which unfortunately proved only too prophetic.

The route, as shown on the map, joined the already overcrowded network in 1894, but by then the age of railways had passed and the age of the 'horseless carriage', or motor car, had begun; still Watkin forged ahead with his plans. His route ran from Beighton in Sheffield to Annesley and thence to Quainton Road in Buckinghamshire, where it was to join the recently extended Metropolitan Railway through to Finchley Road. Here the line would veer off to a new terminus to be named Marylebone, on the site of the former Boscabel Gardens. A last minute setback occurred, however, for when the bill authorising the construction of the line was about to be passed, a sudden dissolution of Parliament caused a postponement of its presentation for a year: Royal permission was eventually granted in 1894.

Obtaining the necessary capital proved far from easy for Watkin as the country was in the middle of a trade depression and he resigned his three directorships in order to raise funds. Lord Wharncliffe succeeded him as Chairman of the MS&L, and together with Alexander Henderson who later joined the board, gave Watkin enough influence to amass sufficient finance. When the contracts had been entered at a cost of £3,132,155, together with £250,000 for the Channel Tunnel project, the board discovered that their budget was probably not going to be enough for all the necessary works to be carried out. The contracts were drawn up divided into six major portions, and one minor portion referring to the section from Canfield Place to Marylebone, as follows:

Section		Length	Contractors
(1)	Annesley-East Leake	19m 44ch	Logan & Hemmingway
(2)	East Leake-Aylestone	16m 36ch	Henry Lovatt
(3)	Aylestone-Rugby	15m 69ch	Topham Jones & Railton
(4)	Rugby-Charwelton	15m 77ch	T. Oliver & Sons
(5)	Charwelton-Brackley	12m 32ch	Walter Scott & Co.
(6)	Brackley-Quainton Rd	12m 61ch	Walter Scott & Co.
(7)	Canfield Place-Marylebone	1m 71ch	J. T. Firbank

Although the standard business rules of price and profit applied to railway companies like the Great Central, they enjoyed two unusual public privileges, namely corporate form and the means to acquire land by compulsory purchase. Despite this useful institution, the Great Central's progress was impeded by some complicated battles over the purchase of land. Of these the greatest was probably the dispute with the cricketers at Lords, whose pitch was dug up for the London Extension. In Northamptonshire, around the future site of Woodford Halse and Charwelton stations, the local landowners were concerned that the railway would upset the beautiful surroundings they lived in and so they also put up considerable resistance. After a series of delicate negotiations some of the original difficulties were resolved by a change in route and the building of a tunnel to hide the railway as it passed Catesby House.

Kellett made the following observations, 'In general the choice of routes, sites and particular operational policies was made privately and according to the ordinary calculations of profitability and investment which prevailed in *laissez-faire* economy. The railway companies were business enterprises floated with private capital and in the long run their success and ultimate survival depended upon the return they were able to give their shareholders. The paramount consideration therefore, in the mind of the projectors and managers of Britain's nineteenth-century railway system when making decisions was a simple one: what balance could be expected between the direct private costs and benefits of investment? The Victorian entrepeneur was guided by common sense and experience raised to a high order not by systems analysis.'

On the basis of the former argument, those who had invested in the Great Central were receiving a far less substantial dividend on their shares than that paid out to Midland subscribers which totalled some sixty per cent, twenty times more than the Great Central's dividend. The latter was due mainly to the draining away of capital on the demolition of houses (£40,000 being spent in London alone) and the hiring of steam plant which cost 20s per day even for the smallest mechanical excavator. Once Watkin had settled the re-housing problem, provided accommodation for foremen and paid for the navvies, the total cost of the London Extension reached £11,500,000.

As well as financial difficulties, the line faced many obstacles created by natural and man-made features which would have daunted earlier railway builders. Undoubtedly the mechanical plant helped lighten the enormity of these tasks. At certain points other companies' lines had to be crossed without disrupting the flow of traffic (for instance the London North Western at Rugby which was fourteen tracks wide, and the Midland at Nottingham where the Great Central went over twelve tracks and the station). In Nottingham and Leicester the spread of industry and housing meant that it was difficult for the London Extension to have a clear run without the demolition of many buildings and the erection of a continuous series of viaducts. In addition, coal extraction in Nottinghamshire led to the line being prone to risks of subsidence or, at least, ground movement.

Besides the magnificent railway structures of Leicester and Nottingham, many notable engineering features could be found along the line: Stanford which bridged the River Soar; Swithland which crossed a large reservoir; Whetstone which carried the line over the River Sence; Braunston, Helmdon, and Brackley a 23-span viaduct which crossed the flood plain where the Ouse rises. From a technical point of view these structures were well built and reinforced to ensure stability, with five layers of asphalt and canvas supporting the track ballast.

In the building of Brackley viaduct, the existence of the flood plain required one of the chief engineers, Sir Douglas Fox, to exercise his skills in reinforcing the structure. This was achieved by incorporating two sets of plate girders and building two retaining walls inside the middle arch. Sadly, the viaduct no longer exists as it was demolished to improve the A43 road, but it didn't go without a fight – it took two attempts to rase it to the ground. Watkin would have been pleased!

Tunnels were an equally important constructional feature of the Great Central. Apart from the necessity to tunnel through or, in the case of cities, under buildings as at Nottingham: Sherwood Rise (662yds), Mansfield Road (1,189yds), Thurland St (600yds) and at London under West Hampstead, St John's Wood and Lords, there were three other tunnels built at East Leake and Dunton Bassett to the south of Ashby Magna station, the third being at Catesby (3,000yds) in Northamptonshire. The latter was technically unnecesary but constructed because the local landowner objected to being able to see the railway. He also imposed restrictions on the siting of the 'breathers' or ventilation shafts. Though Catesby was a shallow-bore tunnel it was not necessary to build it by the 'cut and cover method' which was used on the three tunnels in London to the north of Marylebone.

The permanent way of standard gauge track was laid on a ballasted foundation which was basically made up of large rough stones with coarse gravel, graded into 2in rings on top. Approximately 7,500 cu yds of stone for every mile of double track were required for ballasting and, in addition, engineers made use of burnt clay layers where possible. In Northamptonshire, where ironstone was mined, the slag from this process was used.

In the track, however, there was a strange anomaly in that whereas other companies used 60 and 45ft lengths the Great Central used 30ft sections, changing the tradition even of the Manchester, Sheffield and Lincoln Railway. A modern parallel would have been if British Rail had refused to replace standard track with continuously welded rail because the pre-nationalised four main railway companies had used separate sections of track.

The engineering achievement stands as a tribute to Victorian skill and brute force. A notable example of this is an embankment at Sulgrave which had to be filled with 486,000 cu yds of spoil. Located to the south of Sulgrave, which was served by Helmdon station, the embankment is 43ft high, had slopes of 1 in 3, and was 340ft wide at its base: it covers an area of approximately 17 acres of what had originally been good farmland. Building of the latter features and the skills involved were completely independent of considerations of the viability of the route as a commercial undertaking. Indeed running the line cost effectively was an art in itself where maintenance was concerned, which was borne out by the way stations were built. The local stations were built on the island principle with simple facilities – the island formation allowing one platform to do the work of two by having the up and down main lines running round its two faces. Access to these platforms was gained from the road above or below by a central staircase. So far as the city stations were concerned at Nottingham and Leicester, these had large island platforms with bays at either ends, Nottingham having four, and Leicester having two. Due to constraints on space, two stations in the Nottingham area – at Carrington and Arkwright Street – had to be built in the normal fashion with the tracks running through the centre of the platforms. Three other platforms provided at Rushcliffe Eydon Road and Chacombe Road after the opening of the main line also had to be built in the same way as Arkwright Street and Carrington as the track formation did not allow for island platforms. Because of the island principle the Great Central was able to break with the usual design for larger stations. This included a costly single-span roof which completely enclosed the platforms. However, the Great Central engineers chose a glazed pitched roof with spans of a moderate size rising from the steel columns mounted on the platforms. They defended this departure on the grounds of 'economy of means'. This system allowed for expansion without the disruption that was usually caused by a single-span roof. At Marylebone, which had a three span-roof, plans were formulated for a further expansion which, it was hoped would be justified by the future growth in traffic which, in fact, never materialised. This was one further piece of circumstantial evidence demonstrating the Great Central's questionable viability as an economic enterprise.

Another notable feature of the London Extension was the complete absence of level and farm crossings, which omission made it necessary for bridges to be built at all the locations where the former facilities would be used on other railways. However, the lavish crossings provided for farms and minor roads not only reduced the hazards of the line but it also meant that trains could achieve higher speeds. 'Despite the fact that the engineers had to drive their line across the grain of England and along the very spine of the watershed, there was no gradient steeper than 1 in 176, no curve less than 1 mile radius. To maintain such exacting standards involved extremely heavy engineering works. A succession of deep cuttings alternately with lofty embankments and major structural undertakings making up the pattern of the Great Central.'

Comparatively little has been written about the Great Central, especially on the early years and on its construction. By a happy coincidence a complete pictorial record was made at the time of its construction by a man from Leicester who became really engrossed in the photographing of it and hopefully this will be a suitable tribute to S. W. A. Newton, whose excellent plates are included within.

S. W. A. Newton was born in Leicester at the time when railways were a rapidly expanding form of transport, with new lines appearing all over the place. He became involved with railways in 1894, shortly after having taken on his father's photographic business, when the Great Central began to cut a broad swathe through the city of Leicester. It was during the construction that Newton became infatuated with the line and after a while he decided to leave his home base and travel round recording the advance of the Great Central on its way to London. As the years passed and the Great Central came close to completion, Newton had amassed a substantial number of plates of nearly every large engineering feat, as well as recording the aspects of the social life of the navvies who carried out the construction works with brute force. With his camera Newton captured views of their Mission Society rooms, their living quarters, and included several shots of the navvies themselves at work and at leisure. In fact, Newton covered as many aspects as was humanly possible during the six years of works. Undoubtedly without his work there would have been no record of the construction of England's last 'Great' Main Line Railway.

Even though the London Extension had been completed and officially opened, Newton's task was as yet incomplete since the instigator of the line, Sir Edward Watkin, was to find it necessary to construct two further sections of line in order to generate a through link and a bypass for a rather tortuous traffic bottleneck. The later additions were provided because of the problems created by running south of Quainton. From Quainton to London, the Metropolitan, under John Bell (Chairman), owned the railway and his company was hostile to the Great Central. To the latter the most aggravating element of the quarrel between the two companies was the restriction of the number of trains and delaying tactics imposed on the Great Central by the Metropolitan and because of this the two alternative routes were authorised from Woodford-Banbury and from Neasden-Grendon Underwood (north of Quainton).

The first of the two links cost £300,000 but enabled a better connection to be forged with the Great Western at Banbury. Prior to this, the only way onto the London Extension from the Great Western was via the Princes Risborough-Aylesbury branch. The Banbury-Woodford line had the effect of halving the traffic on the Metropolitan section and was opened in 1900. The partnership with the Great Western for this latter venture was to prove useful to the Great Central as it made the construction of the Neasden-Grendon Underwood 'avoiding line' a more viable concern. Along this route lay Wembley Hill, now Wembley Complex (the land being part of Watkin's estate), where he decided to erect a sort of Eiffel Tower 800ft high. This never got beyond the first stage and is now the site of the football stadium which also had its own railway.

In 1901 Bell stepped down as General Manager of the Metropolitan due to ill health and handed over the office to Charles Ellis, who was the company solicitor. Ellis was aided by Colonel Mellor, the chairman of the Railway. Eventually Sir Sam Fay (the new Great Central Chairman) was able to come to terms with the Metropolitan and resume a full service over the Marylebone-Amersham-Aylesbury section which had previously been the subject of disagreement. The Great Central and Metropolitan later formed a joint committee in 1904 and running rights were leased to the Great Central. Two years later some 50+ miles of track came under the jurisdiction of the Metropolitan and Great Central joint committee.

Harrow South	– Harrow	¼ mile
Harrow	– Rickmansworth	8 miles
Rickmansworth	– Chalfont	4 miles
Chalfont	– Chesham	4 miles
Chalfont	– Aylesbury	16 miles
Aylesbury	– Verney Junction	12 miles
Brill Branch		6 miles

Although the dispute between the Metropolitan and the Great Central was the original reason for building the Metropolitan 'avoiding line' between Neasden and Grendon Underwood Junction, this was to prove an advantage to the Great Central as the trains were often slowed down by local workings and the tortuous trackwork like that south of Aylesbury. The latter was the scene of a fatal accident in December 1904 when an express took a severe curve at speed. On the new section of line there were also a number of striking engineering features in the form of a fly-under at Northolt, a flying junction at Ashendon, and the retaining walls at High Wycombe and Wembley Hill. Newton compiled a vast pictorial collection of all these, up to the time when the line opened to passengers in 1906. Like the London Extension, goods trains started to run a year earlier to test how the new embankments and trackbed would stand up to the weight of trains.

Highlighting the excellence of a massive collection of pictures like S. W. A. Newton's has been difficult but this book has attempted to narrow down the field by using only those views which are suitable for direct comparison. In order to achieve some continuity between the section on construction and the GCR (1976) pictures at the end of the book, some views of the line during its operational life and of the motive power used over the years are included. Apart from the motive power section and that on the preserved stretch of line from Loughborough to Rothley, the more recent pictures taken at the same or similar locations display the line in a state of decay and serve as interesting comparisons with the line as it was originally.

The following pictures are designed to serve as a tribute to both Sir Edward Watkin's and S. W. A. Newton's magnificent undertakings and are a selection of some of the best photographs which were taken over the whole London Extension route. Without the record of the Great Central London Extension's construction, the line would have come and passed without any recognition and, in the words of many of its critics, 'Gone Completely'.

THE LONDON EXTENSION NORTH OF NOTTINGHAM

Beginning at Annesley in Nottinghamshire, the London Extension pursued an interesting course to the city of Nottingham in order to attract traffic from local collieries and afford junctions with other lines in the area. At Annesley itself a massive depot was provided with a marshalling yard for exchanging mineral wagons with the Great Northern Railway. From here the line progressed down to a station at Hucknall which was built on the island principle and had the distinction of having its booking office at street level. Hucknall was also the point of departure for a line to a colliery of that name which provided the Great Central with a staple revenue. After Hucknall, the next station was Bulwell which was a fairly large affair with two important junctions to the north and south of the platform (shown in figs 1 and 2) to the Leen Valley line and the Nottingham and Derby line of the Great Northern. A further station was added with the name Bulwell which was a halt serving the local hall and forest area. Leaving Bulwell, the line reached the outskirts of Nottingham after passing a further junction and exchange sidings for the Great Northern at Bagthorpe. The first station was at New Basford, where the Great Central located its carriage sidings because of the limited space which was available on the Nottingham Victoria site. Other facilities existed south of Nottingham at Arkwright Street, though this depot was soon closed, leaving Annesley and Basford to provide motive power and rolling stock. Between Basford and Nottingham Victoria the line disappeared into tunnels under Sherwood Rise and Mansfield Road, apart from a brief exposure to daylight at Carrington where a station was provided. There was a strange anomaly as, like Nottingham Arkwright Street, this station had to be built of non-standard pattern as far as the Great Central was concerned due to lack of space. Carrington is highlighted by a plan of the station on the following page. At the beginning of the line's history Carrington and Arkwright Street fulfilled an important role. Between 1899 and 1900 they catered for main line trains while Victoria station was being completed. Victoria was always a grand station, as reflected by its name, and boasted some fine features but because it was located in a pit between two tunnels and covered in by massive canopies, it was always difficult to take photographs within its complex. I have included a selection of pictures of the various aspects of the station's finery which is now gone but not forgotten, having been replaced with a soulless shopping centre where, again, it is not easy to take photographs. In addition to the latter development, most of the old Great Central around Nottingham and north as far as Annesley has disappeared with progress and it has been difficult to record a comparison between then and now, so I have detailed the changes and developments below:

Station	Date Opened	Date Closed	Use Today
Arkwright Street	15 Mar 1899	5 May 1969	Part of Housing Estate.
Nottingham Victoria	24 May 1900	4 Sept 1967	Shopping Centre and Bus Station/Depot and Flats.
Carrington	15 Mar 1899	24 Sept 1928	Booking Office is a sweet shop and other buildings are a poodle parlour.
New Basford	15 Mar 1899	7 Sept 1964	Platforms removed with goods shed and yard used for lorry park. Station House is a residence.
Bagthorpe and Basford Carriage Sidings			Housing and Industrial development.
Bulwell Common	15 Mar 1899	4 Mar 1963	Industrial Estate with old station house as a dwelling.
Hucknall	15 Mar 1899	4 Mar 1963	Derelict. Only the station house was occupied when I walked around here.
Annesley Depot	15 Mar 1899	2 Dec 1965	Barely recognisable, with much of the trackbed removed and subsequent building having taken place.

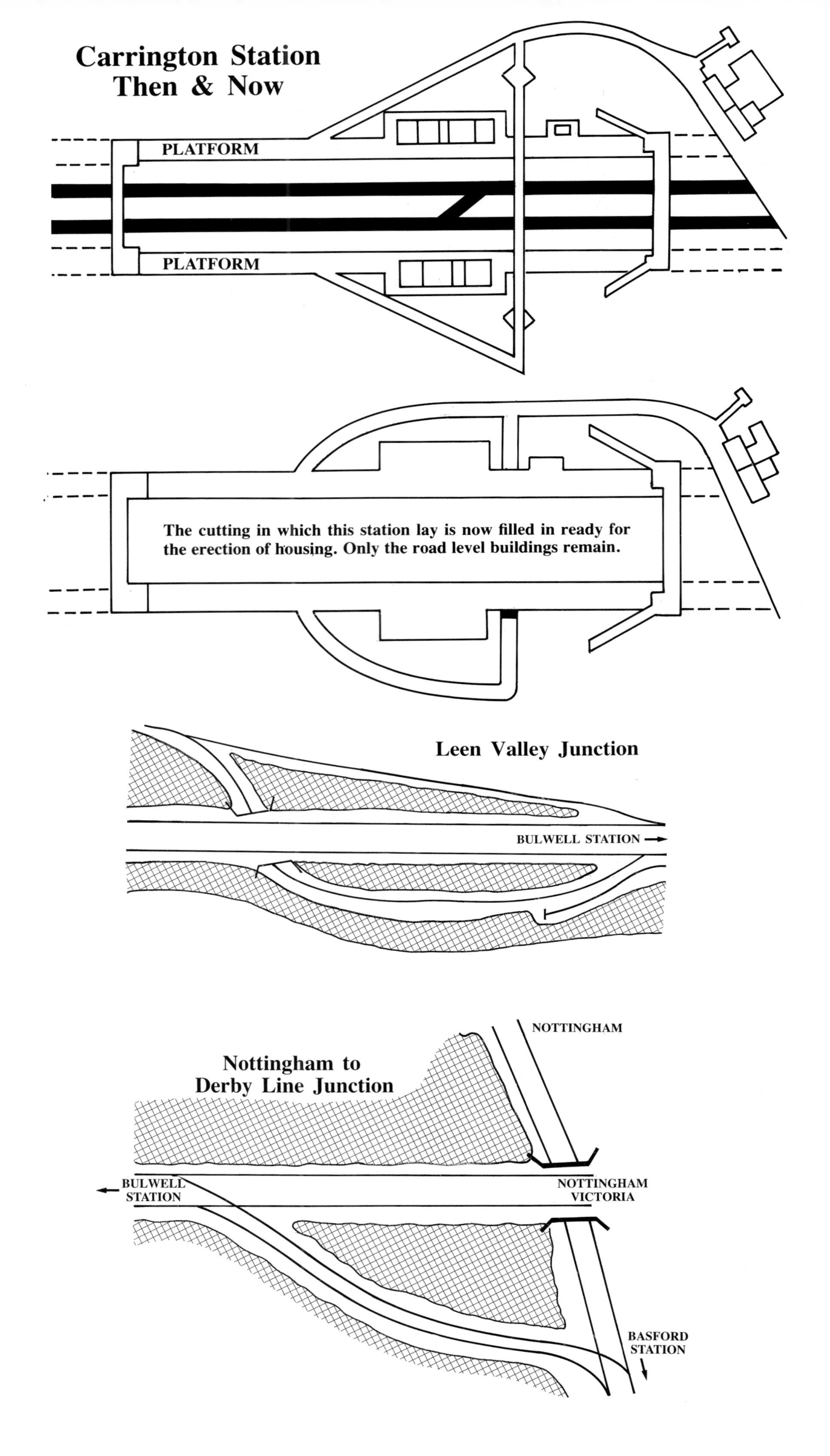
Carrington Station
Then & Now
PLATFORM
PLATFORM
The cutting in which this station lay is now filled in ready for the erection of housing. Only the road level buildings remain.
Leen Valley Junction
BULWELL STATION
Nottingham to
Derby Line Junction
NOTTINGHAM
BULWELL
STATION
NOTTINGHAM
VICTORIA
BASFORD
STATION

A fine view of Nottingham Victoria from Mansfield Road overlooking the station offices, booking hall, clock tower and Great Central Hotel. This scene taken in 1903, three years after opening, has radically changed today as only the clock tower and hotel remain and it is no longer possible to travel from here by train since Victoria is now a haven for shoppers. It is ironic that now Victoria bus station performs the same role as its former railway counterpart.

Inside the booking hall at Nottingham Victoria, where one could buy tickets for a number of destinations ranging from Bournemouth, Swansea, Southampton, London, Rugby, Leicester, Northampton and Grantham to Derby, Shirebrook, Sheffield, Newcastle and all the local stations north and south of the city.

Nottingham Victoria comes alive for the last time as a trunk route, as platform 4 bustles with activity on 3 September 1966 at 12.55 pm. Waiting for its customers is the last through Bournemouth to York train with restaurant car.

A general view of the inside of Nottingham Victoria at platform level in 1903. The buildings in the foreground house the refreshment rooms, while those further down on platforms 4 and 7 cater for the waiting rooms. Access to the platforms is in between, where the clock is mounted on the bridge. This clock had the misfortune to get blackened with smoke and was later removed.

The last through train has departed and tomorrow Nottingham Victoria will become silent save for the rumble of Grantham Diesel Multiple Unit and Rugby local trains. The date is 3 September 1966 and the tranquility of the giant complex says it all.

A rare and famous visitor simmers in platform 10 at Nottingham Victoria with a crowd of onlookers present to see 4472 *Flying Scotsman* which is hauling the GMRS Isle of Wight Special train. In the last years the 'Vic' played host to many special trains, the most celebrated of those being the *East Midlander*.

Demolition is in progress, with the removal of the track through platform 1 and that of the passing loops as well. At this stage only the south bay platforms were used for the Grantham and Rugby services along with the centre roads for goods traffic. Complete closure and demolition followed a few months after this picture was taken, on 4 September 1967.

The tunnel at Mansfield Road at the southern end, completed in 1896 with much progress already evident on the tracklaying through Nottingham Victoria station site. Some 90 years later the bottom photograph shows that the scene has changed little save for the removal of track and the highlighting of the tunnel mouth with a rather witty advertisement for the Nottingham Building Society.

Weekday Cross junction under construction and after demolition. The scene has changed little with the formation of the Grantham line and London route on the right very easily traceable. Gone, sadly, is the signal cabin which was perched in between the two lines as shown in the upper picture. Weekday Cross junction was retained as a head shunt for the line down to East Leake which provided gypsum traffic for British Rail. In 1974 the necessity for the head shunt was avoided with the opening of a new chord from Loughborough Midland to the Great Central which served East Leake and Ruddington. Lifting then took place between Ruddington and Weekday Cross through to Colwick Junction along with the removal of the signal cabin above.

The viaduct across the Trent at Wilford was really one of the most splendid features along the Great Central as it incorporated a mixture of bridge design and remained as a monument to the line long after closure until its sad demolition in 1986. These views show the structure under construction and shortly before its demolition.

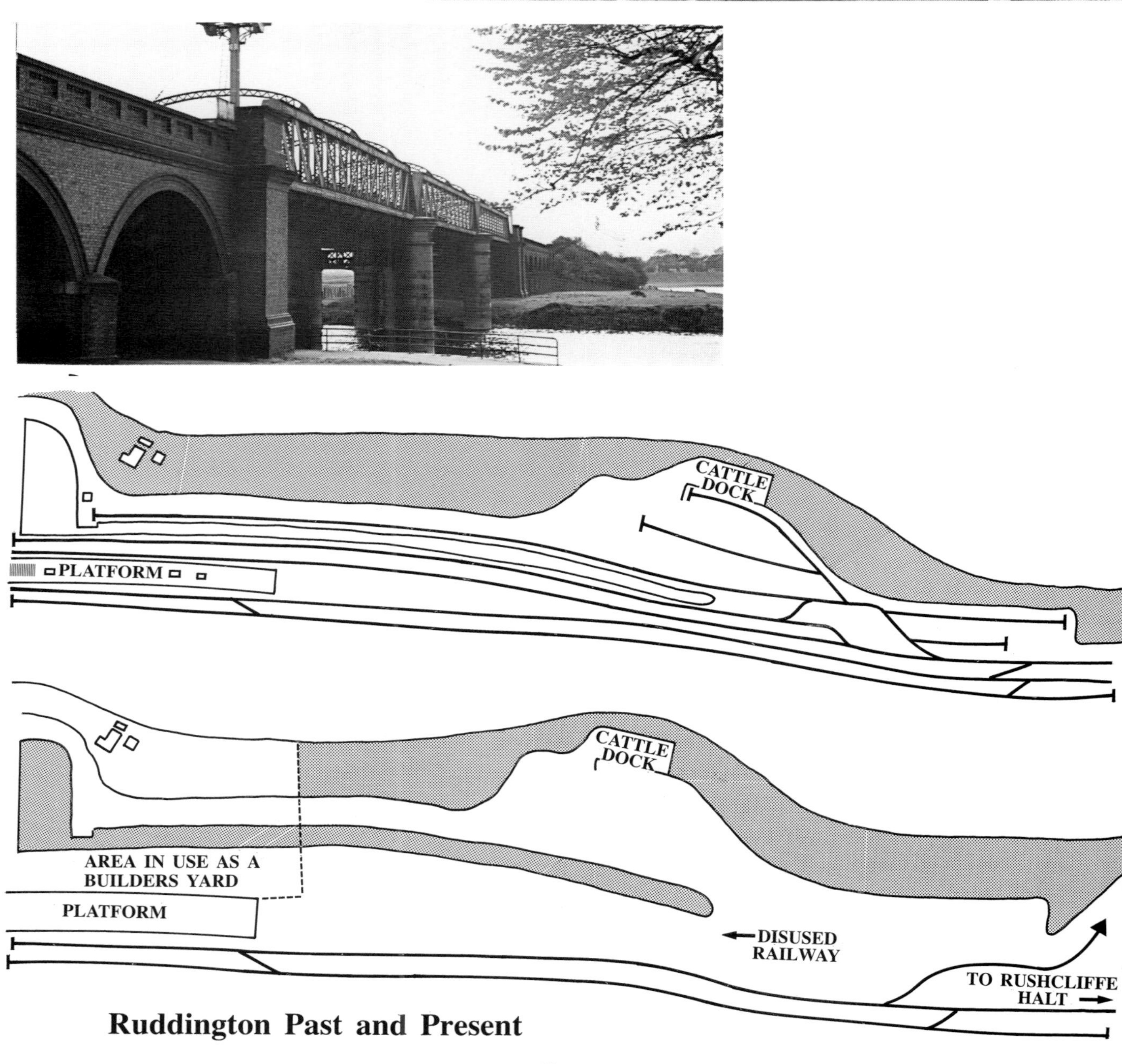

Ruddington Past and Present

MAIN LINE STEAM TRUST

The following section has been omitted from the description of the construction because the stations at Loughborough Central, Quorn and Woodhouse, and Rothley have now become part of the railway preservation scene being run by the two organisations above. Although the basic aim is to try and preserve some of the Great Central, the railway possesses a large selection of fixtures from other companies' lines, as well as a variety of rolling stock. Because of the track laying and alterations to the sites owned by the Great Central Railway 1976, I feel that this particular section of line is not really suitable for comparison with what the railway was once like at Loughborough Central, Quorn and Woodhouse and Rothley, so I have devoted a portion at the end of the book to areas used by the preservation movement. The map below shows the extent of the territory not covered in the description of the construction.

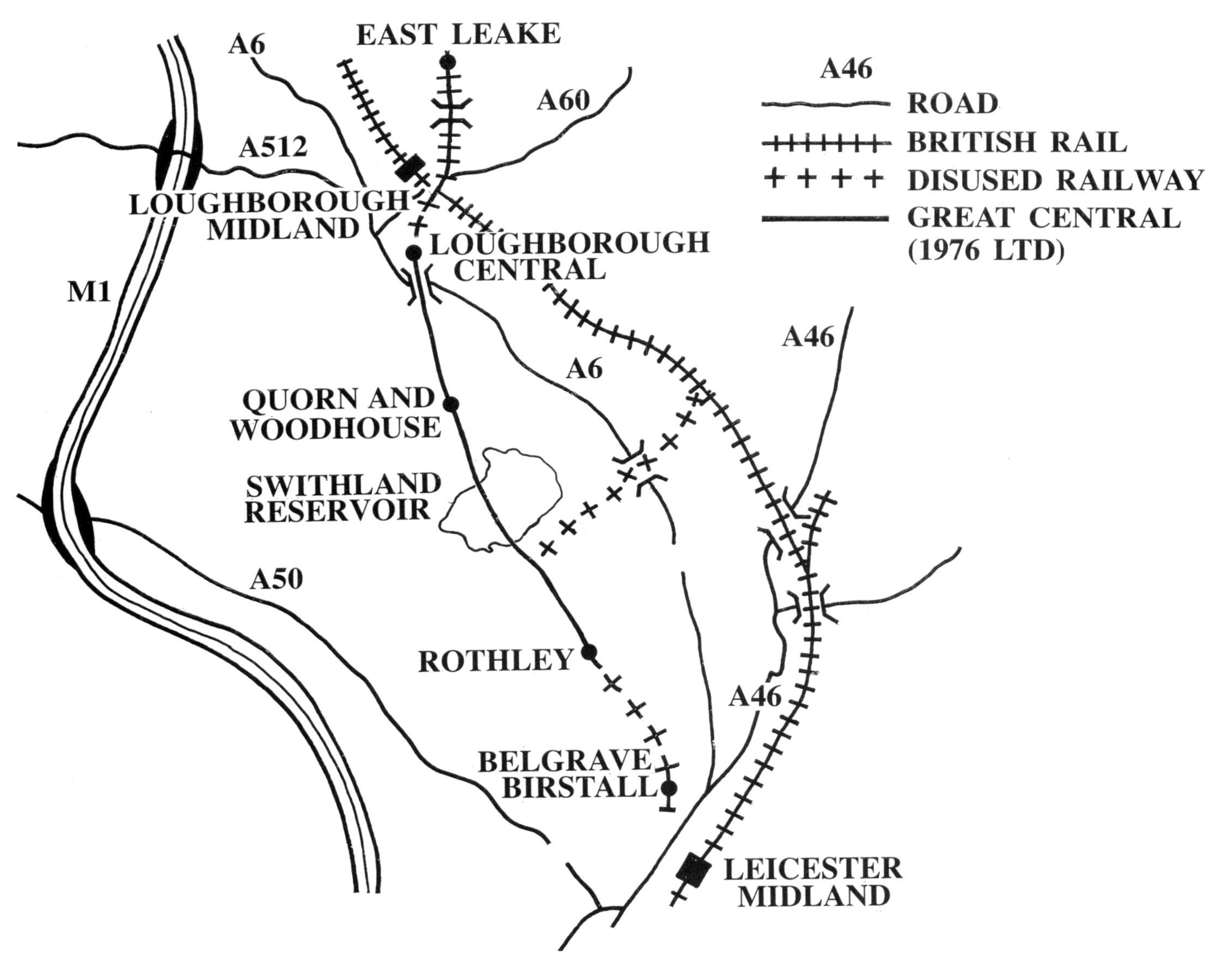

Construction and demolition at Belgrave and Birstall. In the top picture the outline of the station platform can be seen clearly by the positioned edging stones which have yet to be laid by Henry Lovatt & Co. Also at an advanced stage is the construction of the road overbridge. The latter was the only part to remain after the demolition had been carried out by the Main Line Steam Trust on safety grounds, as shown in the lower picture.

Leicester central with the tracks laid and the station almost complete, apart from the canopy. The six platforms were built on a viaduct which was approached through an impressive facade on Great Central Street. Behind it were the booking hall and parcels/ goods office. Under part of the platform the Great Central encountered a Roman pavement which had to be sealed in and this section, along with a few other parts of the old station, are all that remain amidst a development of industrial units and a car park. In the lower picture Leicester is seen a few months before it was reduced to no more than an unstaffed halt, in which state it remained until complete closure and demolition in the 1970s.

Transport Police 'then and now'.

Leicester West Bridge with the finishing touches being put to the girder structure by the navvies, who are using a mixture of plant. At this stage, track laying is a long way off but when the railway opened the series of viaducts through Leicester, of which West Bridge was one, gave people an impressive view of the city. After lifting, the bridge was fortunate to escape the wholesale demolition of the Great Central's structures and became part of the Great Central walkway from Leicester to Aylestone.

Leicester Central engine shed, which is shown nearing completion, lay to the south of the station complex and could accommodate some 30 engines inside. The only tasks remaining for the contractors are to lay the tracks, build the bay window on the shedmaster's office and complete the hanging of the shed doors. These were later removed, as can be seen from the lower picture which shows the shed at a busy period on 12 March 1961. In addition to the alteration to the doors, a flat roof was installed with vents instead of the one shown above.

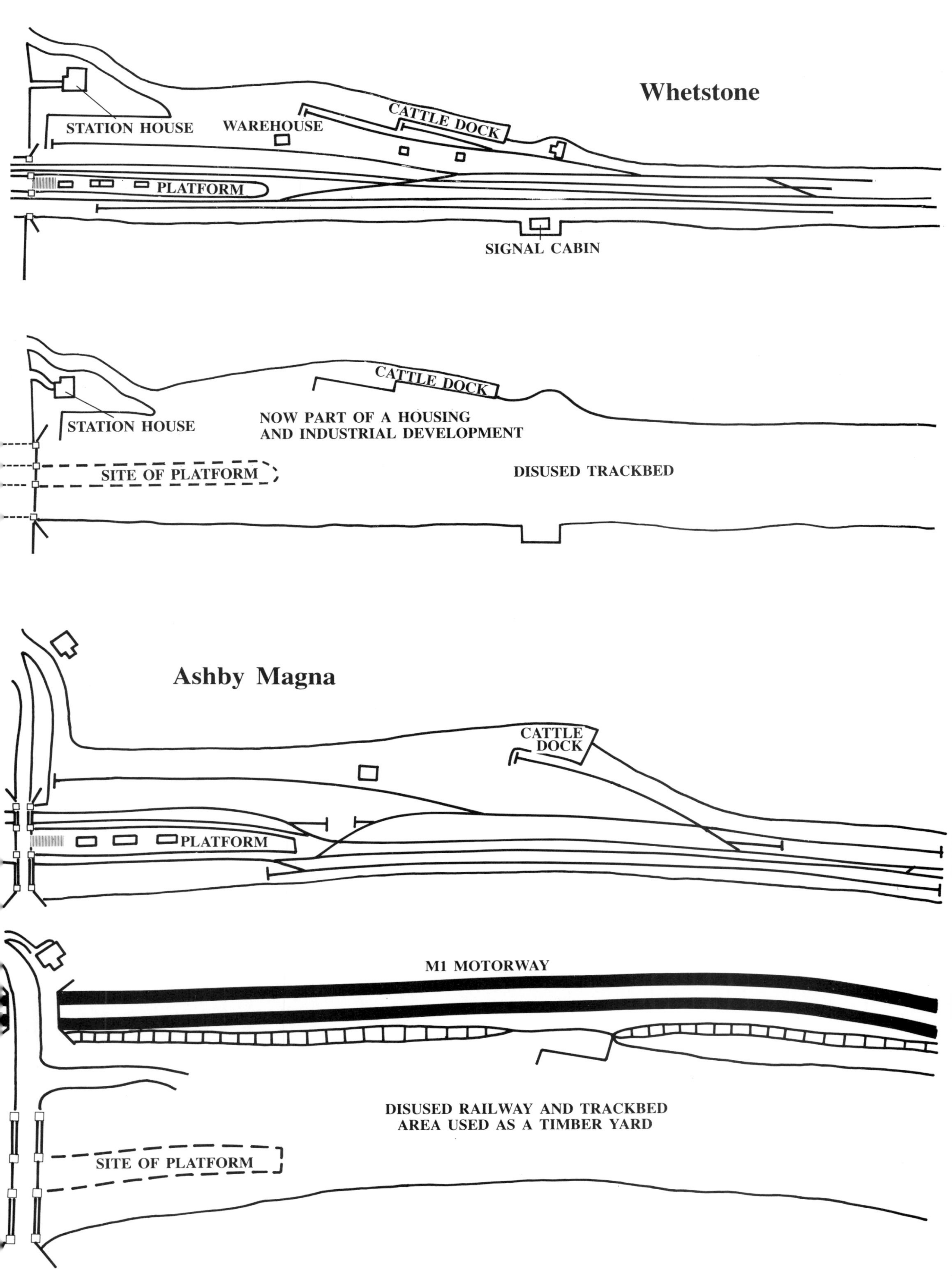
Whetstone
STATION HOUSE
WAREHOUSE
CATTLE DOCK
PLATFORM
SIGNAL CABIN
CATTLE DOCK
STATION HOUSE
NOW PART OF A HOUSING
AND INDUSTRIAL DEVELOPMENT
SITE OF PLATFORM
DISUSED TRACKBED
Ashby Magna
CATTLE
DOCK
PLATFORM
M1 MOTORWAY
DISUSED RAILWAY AND TRACKBED
AREA USED AS A TIMBER YARD
SITE OF PLATFORM

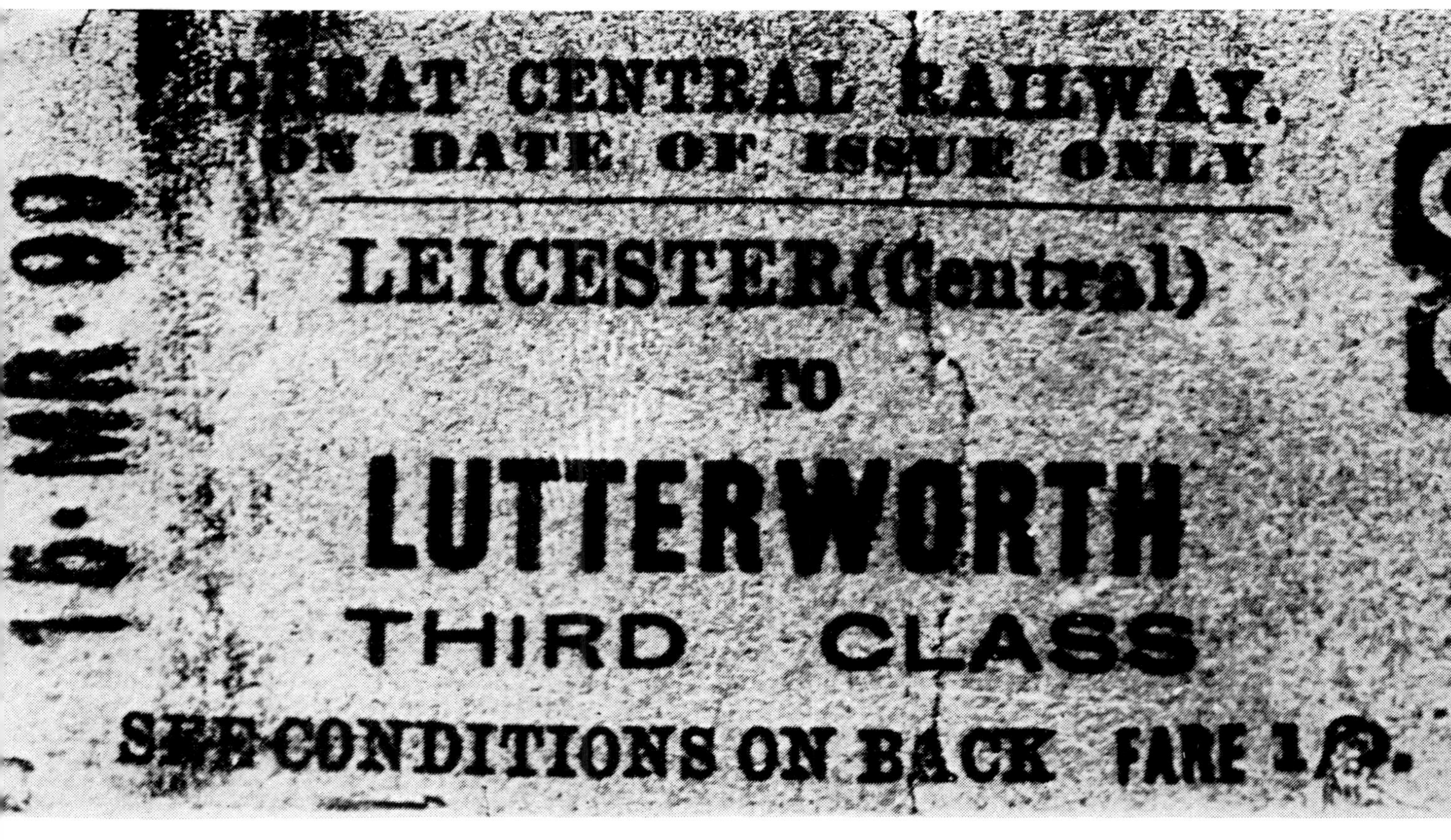

Lutterworth and a third class single ticket from Leicester Central valid for the first day of Great Central London Extension services. Note the fare which is 1d, compared to the £1.60 on the modern equivalent for the same distance.

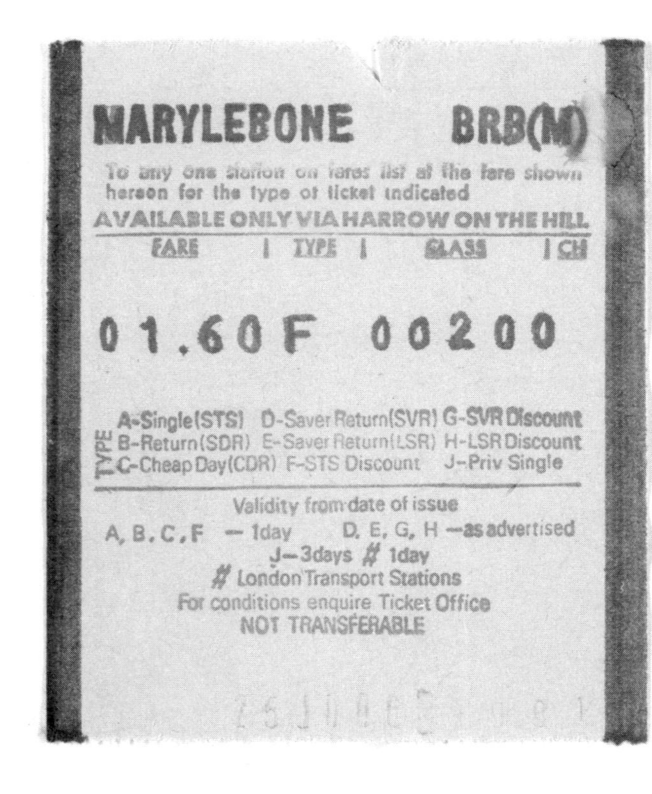

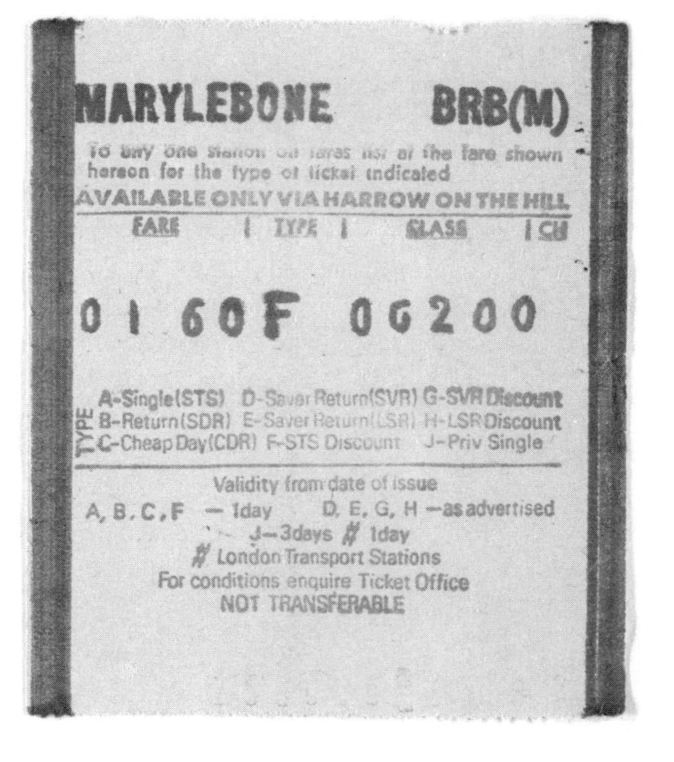

Rugby Central, the day before pasenger services started on 15 March 1899, looking a fine spectacle of a station. This was one of the larger platforms on the London Extension; Brackley, Woodford Halse, Leicester, Loughborough and Nottingham being the others. Note the elaborate booking hall building and the access to the platforms. Sadly, all this has now gone, having been demolished in 1970 when the lower photograph was taken.

A fortunate survivor is Braunston and Willoughby station house. In railway days the stationmaster, who is pictured above in front of the house, was generally regarded with esteem and was provided with lavish accommodation at every location. The lower picture shows Brackley as a private dwelling today.

Catesby Tunnel from the north end, with work fairly advanced on the cuttings leading up to the tunnel portal which lay under the home of the gunpowder plotter Robert Catesby. The bricks on the left are for lining the tunnel and facing the entrance to the tunnel which, even today, though devoid of tracks remains remarkably intact as a monument to Victorian skill.

Eighty-three years have elapsed between these two pictures and there is little change at Catesby Tunnel, save for the removal of the railway and the encroachment of nature, but a haunting mist and sounds of steam engines still emanate from the northern portal.

Charwelton station entrance and booking office during a visit by the royal train in 1909. In the lower photograph, the platform has been removed and the bridge which carries the A361 awaits demolition to allow much needed road improvements.

Woodford Halse North Curve Junction shortly after the opening of the London Extension, showing the station and goods yard in the background. From the same viewpoint today, the trackbed is easily definable, for only nature has taken over this area.

On a wet day in 1920 the camera catches a shot of a deserted island platform and goods yard at Culworth. Note the proud boast above the waiting room sign that the station has a telephone. Today, the station site is used as a farm, with only the building on the right remaining.

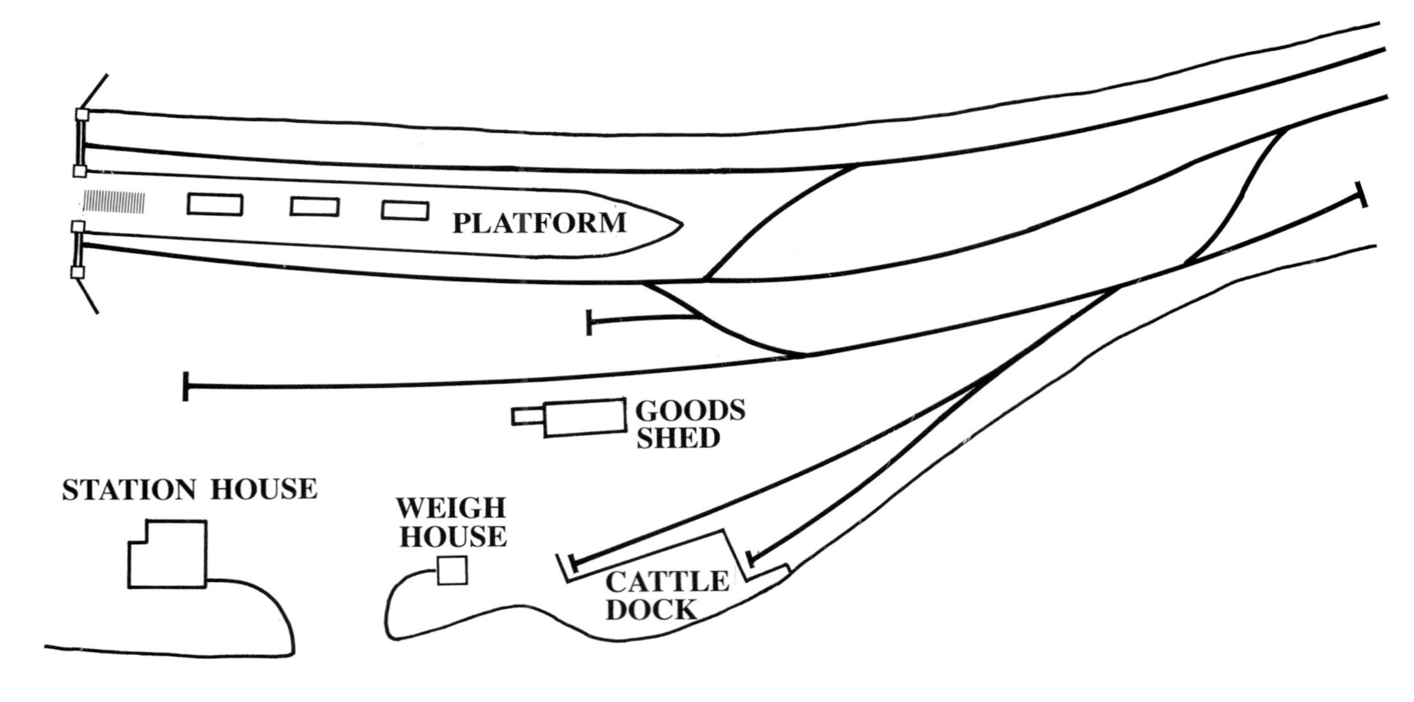

Helmdon Then and Now

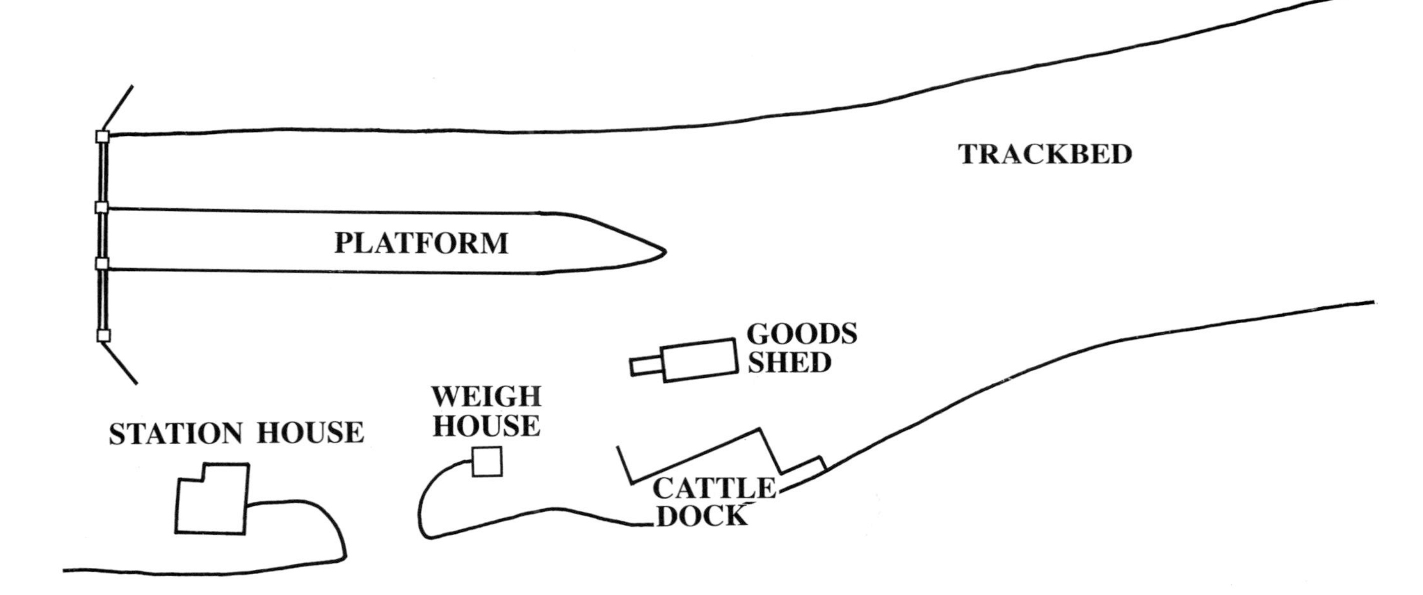

How times have changed in these two photographs of Brackley Central, with the one above showing the station on 9 March 1899 with a crowd of well-wishers waiting to herald the arrival of the first train from Nottingham, which is just coming under the bridge. The bridge became a casualty of improvements to the main road and no longer exists, and the platform area has been built over. Only the booking office remains, as seen in the lower picture.

An elaborate farm crossing just north of Finmere which has changed very little since construction save for the encroachment of greenery.

Calvert was the last port of call on the London Extension and in this picture the road overbridge is complete, leaving the entrance to the platform and the buildings to be built. Though the station is closed and the buildings are gone, the tracks of both former main lines are in use as a siding and for through freight traffic from the Bletchley to Oxford line.

Another view of Calvert station in the 1920s looking over the island platform and goods yard. The scene has drastically altered due to the lifting of the goods yard and demolition of the station buildings.

Upper South Farm Junction then and now, at one time the start of the Great Central London Extension to Annesley and now just a single track line with no evidence of the existence of a once important junction.

Quainton Road station looking towards the Great Central junction with the Metropolitan. Quainton was once regarded as the Clapham Junction of the north. Today its role is somewhat different, being part of the Buckinghamshire Steam Centre. The line on the right is used for freight between Aylesbury and Bletchley.

THE WYCOMBE ROUTE

Originally the Great Central intended to rely heavily on running its trains over Metropolitan metals from Quainton Road to Marylebone, but there were a number of drawbacks in that speed was a problem near Aylesbury due to the tortuous nature of the approach to the station. The latter was borne out by the fatal accident of December 1904. Consideration also had to be given to the routing of London Extension expresses over what was an already crowded system. Initially these difficulties posed no significant problems and both companies were able to run over shared tracks with little cause for any aggravation.

However, the friendly agreement did not last for long and a dispute erupted between Sir Edward Watkin and John Bell, Chairman of the Metropolitan. The Metropolitan employed all kinds of tactics, including the holding of trains and, in one instance, refused to allow the train to pass. A quick solution had to be found for the London Extension and a golden opportunity arose which would benefit the Great Western and Great Central Railways. The scheme that was negotiated stated that the Great Central would share the cost in rebuilding the Wycombe Railway between High Wycombe and Princes Risborough, while in return the Great Western promised to help build a new line from Northolt to High Wycombe to allow the Great Central access to Marylebone by building its own link from Northolt to Neasden and thence to London. The Great Western, on the other hand, used this new plan to link Northolt with Acton on their main line.

Construction work began as soon as possible and the line was opened to passenger traffic on 2 April 1906 as far as Grendon Underwood junction, situated between Quainton Road and Calvert. With the avoiding line complete, the majority of long-distance express working was routed via High Wycombe until 1960, when the semi-fasts from Marylebone to Nottingham used the Amersham to Aylesbury route.

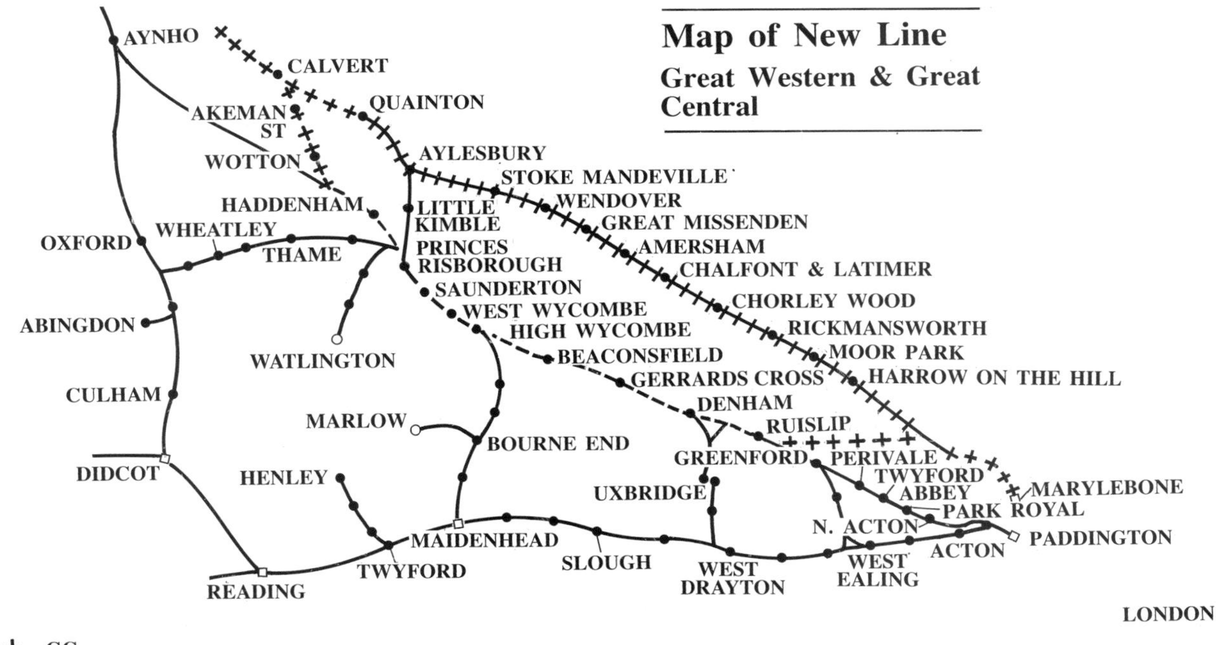

Princes Risborough at the time of construction of the joint Great Western/ Great Central line to Grendon Underwood. Originally the station had been a simple stopping place on the Wycombe to Aylesbury and Thame/ Oxford lines, but the arrival of the Great Central turned the station into a major junction of great importance. The lower picture shows the station prior to the start of a reduction in services. Today the platforms have been reduced to two and the track layout drastically rationalised.

Near Wycombe at the time of rebuilding (above) and (below) 62666 *Zeebrugge* works the Northern Rubber Special past the same spot in June 1963. The signal cabin has been demolished but steam trains can still be seen in this area on certain Sundays when working the Sunday Luncheon Pullman services to Stratford-upon-Avon.

Wembley Park station in the final stages of construction has gone through three changes of name: Wembley Hill, Wembley Complex and is now Wembley Stadium. It is little more than an unstaffed halt serving the stadium, arena and conference centre.

Marylebone station past and present.

The navvies who built the line posing
with the tools of their trade: hand
implements and mechanical excavators.

The navvies at work and at leisure.

MOTIVE POWER

Motive power for different purposes with contractors' engine *Llanelly* (above) photographed in 1896, while below, some ten years later, the locomotive crew are seen posing in front of 8B *Atlantic* 867 at Woodford Halse. The latter were the mainstay of motive power on the London Extension in the early years.

At the end of the Great Central's ownership of the London Extension, one of the best performers was the 'Director' Class out of which one has fortunately been preserved by the Great Central Railway, Loughborough, this being No. 506 *Butler Henderson* (above). Most of the latter class were absorbed by the London North Eastern Railway at grouping though it was apparent that new motive power would be required and this was provided by the B17 'Footballer' Class, No. 2866 *Nottingham Forest* being one of this type (lower).

During London North Eastern Railway control the Great Central saw many of its engines adorned in the latter company's livery, as the above picture of a D9 shows. In 1947 the line was nationalised but, in general, the locomotives comprised of ex-Eastern Railway stock and Great Central varieties and it was not until the change in regional control in 1958 that many ex-Midland types began to appear, as shown in the lower picture of Woodford Halse where LMS 8F 8121 stands alongside a BR standard 5 No. 73010 and an unidentified Great Western Hall.

Even in the Diesel Multiple Unit era there have been changes, as shown in these views of Aylesbury Town. When the above photograph was taken the engine shed was still in evidence and trains still ran to Nottingham Victoria, which is where the train in platform 3 is destined for. Nowadays the units, dressed in a different livery, finish their journey at Aylesbury, apart from the odd special which affords passengers the chance to travel north of Buckinghamshire's county town. One such train was a shopper's special to Milton Keynes organised by the author, and pictured below.

Finmere Permanent Way and not so
permanent way!

Brackley Station exterior in August 1966, a month before railway operation ceased, and some twenty years later in August 1986; fortunately the booking office survives and has only had minor alterations made to it to cater for its present use as an exhaust and tyre centre.

Leaving Woodford Halse on the last day of operation is 44984 with the final day working to Marylebone on 3 September 1966. The scene has considerably changed mainly because of the removal of the permanent way.

Woodford and Hinton station later became Woodford Halse, seen in these two photographs in its heyday, and at the end of its life in the lower picture. Gone are the yards and the Banbury local service leaving only the semi-fasts and cross-country services to call at Woodford's forlorn looking island platform.

Woodford Halse locomotive depot before and after closure. The lower view, taken in 1968, has changed considerably as the sheds were rased to the ground and the area has subsequently been developed as an industrial complex.

Charwelton showing the striking comparison between a busy country station with a local train departing and a number of ironstone wagons in the yard and a vast expanse of derelict land. Since the lower picture was taken, road improvements have obliterated the bridge in the background and the remains of the platform.

Catesby Tunnel southern end, which was the lead up to Charwelton station, past and present.

Catesby Tunnel, southern end, Permanent Way and not so permanent way.

Only three years separate these two shots of Leicester Central, the first depicting a Nottingham to Marylebone parcels train picking up vans from the south bay at the station, while the second, taken from a Nottingham to Rugby Central DMU in 1967, shows how the north bay has suffered decay with the withdrawal of most of the services. Today the area is used as a car park and industrial estate.

Leicester Central shed before and after closure.

The same passenger diagram: the Newcastle to Bournemouth train being worked by steam and diesel into Leicester Central on 14 July 1946 and 2 September 1966 respectively. The Great Central was never to enjoy the full benefits of any modernisation and new motive power, because the line closed as a trunk route on the day after the lower photograph was taken.

One of the more interesting points on the London Extension was Weekday Cross, the junction for the Grantham line which led off to the right. In the above picture 61159 B1 Class thunders through the southern portal of the tunnel with the *South Yorkshireman*. Now devoid of track, the tunnel to Nottingham Victoria carries heating pipes for the new shopping centre built on the site of the old station.

Without doubt the most splendid station on the London Extension was Nottingham Victoria, renowned for its tasteful construction, as shown in the picture above, where 30925 *Cheltenham* and 2P 40646 are seen standing in platform 4 with the RCTS *East Midlander*. It is hard to believe that the lower picture is the same view twenty years on, dominated by the soulless concrete slab in the background which replaced the station.

The north end of Nottingham Victoria station then and now.

Cancels Handbill AD136

Train Service

Nottingham Arkwright Street and Rugby Central.

on and from 1 January 1968 the following service will operate.

				SO			SX
NOTTINGHAM Arkwright St. dep.	07 50	08 22	12 27	13 55	16 17	17 34	18 52
EAST LEAKE ... ... dep.	08 03	08 35	12 40	14 08	16 30	17 47	19 05
LOUGHBOROUGH Central arr.	08 10	08 42	12 47	14 15	16 37	17 54	19 12
" " ... dep.	08 11	08 43	12 48	14 16	16 38	17 55	19 13
LEICESTER Central ... ... arr.	08 24	08 56	13 01	14 29	16 51	18 08	19 26
" " ... ... dep.	08 26	08 58	13 03	14 31	16 53	18 10	19 28
ASHBY MAGNA ... ... dep.	08 41	09 13	13 18	14 46	17 08	18 25	19 43
LUTTERWORTH ... ... dep.	08 48	09 20	13 25	14 53	17 15	18 32	19 50
RUGBY Central ... ... arr.	08 57	09 29	13 34	15 02	17 24	18 41	19 59

				SO			SX	
RUGBY Central ... ... dep.	—	07 11	10 30	12 30	15 05	16 20	17 37	18 55
LUTTERWORTH ... ... dep.	—	07 20	10 39	12 39	15 14	16 29	17 46	19 04
ASHBY MAGNA ... ... dep.	—	07 28	10 47	12 47	15 22	16 37	17 54	19 12
LEICESTER Central ... ... arr.	—	07 41	11 00	13 00	15 35	16 50	18 07	19 25
" " ... ... dep.	07 10	07 43	11 02	13 05	15 37	16 55	18 12	19 30
LOUGHBOROUGH Central arr.	07 21	07 54	11 13	13 16	15 48	17 06	18 23	19 41
" " ... dep.	07 22	07 55	11 14	13 17	15 49	17 07	18 24	19 42
EAST LEAKE ... ... dep.	07 30	08 03	11 22	13 25	15 57	17 15	18 32	19 50
NOTTINGHAM Arkwright St. arr.	07 42	08 15	11 34	13 37	16 09	17 27	18 44	20 02

Notes: SO—Saturday only. SX—Saturdays excepted.

This service will provide SECOND CLASS accommodation only.

Passengers will be able to obtain tickets, **between stations served by this Service only,** from the Guard in charge of the train.

Accommodation will be provided for the conveyance of cycles, perambulators, etc., accompanied by passengers, who will be responsible for the removal of these articles from the stations.

Unaccompanied traffic will not be conveyed.

Season tickets, **between stations served by the Service only,** will be issued at Nottingham Midland, Leicester London Road and Rugby Midland Stations.

From:	Nottingham		East Leake		Loughboro Cen.		Leicester Central		Ashby Magna		Lutterworth		Rugby Central	
To:	S	R	S	R	S	R	S	R	S	R	S	R	S	R
Nottingham ...	–	–	2/6	3/9	3/9	5/–	6/3	7/6	8/9	11/–	9/9	13/6	11/9	16/–
East Leake	2/6	3/9	–	–	1/4	2/6	4/3	5/6	6/6	10/–	7/9	12/–	9/6	14/6
Loughboro Central	3/9	5/–	1/4	2/6	–	–	2/9	4/6	5/6	9/–	6/3	11/3	8/3	14/3
Leicester Central ...	6/3	7/6	4/3	5/6	2/9	4/6	–	–	2/9	4/9	4/–	6/3	5/6	9/–
Ashby Magna ...	8/9	11/–	6/6	10/–	5/6	9/–	2/9	4/9	–	–	1/2	2/3	3/–	5/6
Lutterworth ...	9/9	13/6	7/9	12/–	6/3	11/3	4/–	6/3	1/2	2/3	–	–	2/–	3/9
Rugby Central ...	11/9	16/–	9/6	14/6	8/3	14/3	5/6	9/–	3/–	5/6	2/–	3/9	–	–

The return fare quoted above is that for Cheap Day Return.

London Midland Region

Issued by British Railways
Divisional Manager, Furlong House,
Middle Furlong Road, Nottingham.

AD136X BR 35000 December, 1967

The December 1967 handbill relating to the last vestige of any kind of service on the Great Central between Rugby and Nottingham which was reduced to pay train status on 3 September 1966 and lasted until 5 May 1969.

WITHDRAWAL OF PASSENGER TRAIN SERVICES

BETWEEN

NOTTINGHAM ARKWRIGHT STREET

AND

RUGBY CENTRAL

Following the consent of the Minister of Transport, the passenger train services will be withdrawn and the following stations CLOSED on and from Monday, 5th May, 1969; subject to the Traffic Commissioners for the East Midland and the West Midland areas granting licences for the operation of additional and revised bus services.

ASHBY MAGNA
EAST LEAKE
LEICESTER CENTRAL
LOUGHBOROUGH CENTRAL
LUTTERWORTH
NOTTINGHAM ARKWRIGHT STREET
RUGBY CENTRAL

REVISED SERVICE :
SOUTH NOTTS BUS CO. LTD.
SERVICE — LOUGHBOROUGH TO NOTTINGHAM VIA EAST LEAKE

MONDAYS TO FRIDAYS

The 18.30 departure from Loughborough (Bus Station) will be retimed to depart at 18.35. The new timings for this journey will be:—

Loughborough (Bus Station)	18.35
Stanford-on-Soar (Church)	18.42
East Leake (Kirk Lea)	18.50
Gotham (Garage)	19.00
Barton Lodge	—
Clifton Pastures	19.06
Clifton Green	19.09
Wilford Green	19.14
Nottingham (Huntingdon Street) ...	19.25

N.B. The 18.30 journey from Loughborough to Nottingham on SATURDAYS will NOT be retimed.

See over for additional bus services between Rugby and Leicester.

BR 35001 March 1969 AD197

From railways to roads: the withdrawal of passenger services on the last remaining portion of the London Extension is scheduled, after which time the local areas will be catered for by buses not trains.

Bulwell Common from both ends of the station in its heyday and after removal of the station buildings. Bulwell was once an important exchange point for two junctions, hence the number of sidings at the complex. These remained in use until 25 May 1968, catering for trains running through Nottingham Victoria to Annesley carrying freight. In the lower picture partial removal has begun though most of the tracks are still in evidence a year after closure. The train in the foreground is a track recovery working, which is on its way from the Leen Valley-Derby line to Bagthorpe Junction, whence it would have travelled round to Nottingham Midland via Gedling.

Marylebone station, the terminus of present-day operations from the truncated lines to Banbury and Aylesbury, as seen from the exterior in June 1984.

The canopy between the terminus at Marylebone and the former Great Central Hotel which up until recently was the headquarters of British Railways, and is now destined to become a luxury hotel again. Note the old fashioned London Taxi by the station entrance which was being used for filming purposes.

Marylebone looking towards Lords Tunnel and the north, with a Banbury train signalled for departure. On the left, the large concrete slab betrays the site of the former station platform signal cabin.

Taken from platform 1 of Marylebone station a newly refurbished Diesel Multiple Unit stands in the stabling siding on 8 June 1984, the day before it worked the *Milton Keynes Shopper* special which was run via Wycombe, Aylesbury, Quainton Road, Winslow and Bletchley.

Under the canopy at Marylebone, the 13.10 Diesel Multiple Unit service to Aylesbury simmers gently as it waits to depart. When this picture of the station was taken the station's future was far from certain; it was under threat of closure.

Looking north is the Diesel Multiple Unit depot on the right in the background, and the station throat is in the foreground, which once was busy with the passage of both express and local trains, though now it is reduced to the rumbings of a humble commuter service. Evidence of Marylebone's former importance can be seen on the left under the bridge with the turntable.

Marylebone was lucky to have a turntable and to be an underused station which made it an ideal location for the running of steam specials which made a welcome return on 12 January 1985. In the top picture, on 26 January 1985 4498 *Sir Nigel Gresley* is coaling up ready to haul the Thames Avon Pullman to Stratford-upon-Avon.

As time went on, the Sunday luncheon specials from Marylebone became more popular and it was decided to run a regular service with varied motive power. In this picture, 35028 *Clan Line* in pristine condition sits in platform 4 with the *Shakespeare Limited* for Stratford-upon-Avon.

46299 *Duchess of Hamilton* adorned with *Shakespeare Limited* headboard stands in platform 3 at Marylebone, on display for all to see in July 1985. Unfortunately, the engine which worked a number of excursions proved unsuitable for the route and has not been used since, giving way to *Sir Lamiel* No. 777.

Steam meets diesel at Marylebone on 7 July 1985 with 'Merchant Navy' class 35028 *Clan Line* on the left, and an unidentified Diesel Multiple Unit on the right bound for Aylesbury. In addition to *Clan Line*, other famous engines including *City of Wells* 34092, *Flying Scotsman* 4472, *Mallard* 4468 and *Green Arrow* 4771 have worked out of Marylebone on numerous Pullmans or *Shakespeare Limited* trains.

BRITISH RAILWAYS BOARD

PUBLIC NOTICE

The British Railways Board has decided not to proceed with the proposal to discontinue all railway passenger services between Marylebone and Harrow-on-the-Hill South Junction, and between Neasden South and Northolt Junction East, and from the following stations:—

London (Marylebone)
Wembley Complex
Sudbury & Harrow Road
Sudbury Hill, Harrow
Northolt Park

also all BR passenger services from the following stations:—

Harrow-on-the-Hill
Moor Park
Rickmansworth
Chorley Wood
Chalfont & Latimer

Any enquiries regarding the above to be made to:—

London & South East Business Manager
London Midland Region
Melbury House
Melbury Terrace
LONDON NW1 6JU

Director, London & South East
Waterloo Station
LONDON SE1 8SE

30th April 1986

Following the success of the steam trains and increased passenger loading due to the creation of the Network South East sector, British Rail has abandoned its intentions to close Marylebone, the last major outpost of the Great Central London Extension.

THE PRESERVED GCR LINE

On 20 May 1973 Loughborough Central station is seen from the road overbridge as being a hive of activity. At this stage operations were limited to brakevan rides up and down the station yard, which were provided in the main by the tank engines in the foreground, save for *Robert Nelson No. 4* which was in the process of restoration. The other three, from right to left, are *Marston Thompson and Evershed No. 3*, No. 39, and *Lamport No. 3*. *Lamport* and No. 39 have now left the railway and are at Market Bosworth and Carnforth respectively.

The signal cabin at Loughborough which has been lovingly restored with equipment from Ruddington, shortly after the Great Central began operations to Quorn and Woodhouse. Since this time, a complete programme of signalling works now means that the box controls the line as far as south of Loughborough Central station, as well as being the focal point for the railway's telephone system.

Restoration in progress, beginning and end, with B1 61264 in pieces and stripped down to its frames in the upper picture, while below another restoration project requires the finishing touches before it can enter service. The J94 was subsequently numbered 68009 and inscribed on either side of its tanks with the words British Railways.

Foreign and British motive power, with the mainstay of the Main Line Steam Trusts early services, *King Haakon VII* No. 377 of the Norwegian State Railways sitting in front of what was later to become the locomotive shed area. Below 5205 class No. 5224 waits to work away from Loughborough on Easter Monday 1985, displaying the fine transformation of what was a rusting hulk into a beautiful workhorse.

Motive power at Loughborough Central with *Robert Nelson No. 4* waiting to depart on a Rothley working in January 1986 from Loughborough Central, (above) while (below) LNER 4744, owned by the Gresley Society, waits to depart bunker first on an afternoon train to Rothley on Easter Sunday 1986. Note the difference in the size of the two engines and the condensing apparatus on the London North Eastern tank.

Quorn and Woodhouse station which has changed very little over the years, apart from a short spell when it lay out of service. The station name is still neatly maintained in the bank by the down platform, while the goods yard is used as a picnic site and for a gala event on Easter weekends. In the lower picture the entrance and booking office are a fine example of the dedicated restoration work that has been effected; to add a touch of realism there is an original Great Central Barnum coach in the background.

Quorn and Woodhouse (above) prior to takeover by the Main Line Steam Trust in 1970 and in a sorry state of repair and (below) once again a hive of activity on Easter weekend 1985, seen from the up side of the platform which at this stage was the only track through the station, as the down line in the upper picture was removed in 1976, due to the Main Line Steam Trust having insufficient funds to purchase it.

An overall view of activities at Quorn and Woodhouse station on Easter weekend 1985, with a train having just pulled in from Loughborough Central which is bringing more passengers to the Road Rail Steam event. On the left is the funfair, restaurant facility, the large steam crane currently lifting a tank wagon and the *Duke of Gloucester* engine; while on the right is the station platform and buildings. (below) Only one building is in need of restoration and that is the signal cabin which is crucial to the development of the site as it will when complete, allow for two-train operation and expansion in the yard below.

Steaming gently at Quorn and Woodhouse, *Robert Nelson No. 4* departs from platform 1 with a winter service to Rothley. In summer, when the passenger loadings are heavier, the railway uses bigger engines such as B1 1306 *Mayflower* which is seen in the picture below pulling into Rothley, the terminus of Great Central Railway operations at present.

Looking towards Belgrave and Birstall which is eventually to become the limit of operations to the south, with many construction materials in evidence. Note the superpower employed on the train which has just pulled in from Quorn and Woodhouse, the engines being No. 506 *Butler Henderson* at the front and LNER N2 tank No. 4744. In the lower picture, later in 1986, *Robert Nelson* is sitting under the road overbridge at Rothley waiting to head back to Loughborough with the last train of the day.

POSTSCRIPT

This volume has touched upon only part of the Great Central, namely the London Extension which was considered to be the most significant development in the history of British Railways, being part of a dream to link Manchester with Paris by a series of lines and a Channel Tunnel. The significance of the route was further enhanced by it being the last main line to be built and the fact that it was one of the few railways to have been comprehensively chronicled during its construction.

It could be said that the London Extension was doomed from the beginning as it arrived after the boom in railway building was effectively over, at a time when the emergence of the 'horseless carriage', or motor car, was becoming more and more evident. Despite its critics, the Manchester Sheffield and Lincoln Railway (later the Great Central), under Sir Edward Watkin, fought back valiantly both with the competition from the car and the motor lorry as well as struggling with the other main railway companies who had been opposed to the arrival of yet another new line to London. It was not until the late fifties that the pinch was felt as the then massive state-owned railway network was using its resources to prop up a system that was in dire need of modernisation. It was also losing a substantial amount of revenue as more and more people began to afford private transport, with the result that subsequent government investment was directed towards building better roads. In the Great Central's case, road competition and state ownership was to be the last straw, as the line had always been an economic balancing act which had been kept steady only by careful management.

The situation changed as early as 1958 when the line was transferred from the Eastern Region of British Railways to the Midland Region. The Midland Region already had lines serving Leicester, Rugby, Nottingham and Sheffield/ Manchester, so the Great Central was dubbed a duplicate main line and was therefore considered no longer essential to the economic performance of the British Railways system. This view was based on the fact that the Great Central had located many of its stations in areas where the population was very sparse. Also, the line from Marylebone, unlike its counterpart from St Pancras was not well linked to other parts of the system, except at Banbury and in the Nottingham area. On the other hand, the Great Central did have several strategic advantages which were overlooked at the time the Beeching Report was carried out. It was the newest line to be built using modern techniques and it avoided all the hazards which were encountered by other companies, for example, level crossings and elaborate station buildings. However, this attention to speed and thrift was not enough to save Sir Edward Watkin's monument when the Beeching Axe fell.

In 1958, with the change in regional control for the old Great Central route, operating policies were disrupted by the introduction of different procedures which aggravated the men. Coupled to this was the gradual removal of the line's best engines such as the V2 class, which became necessary because spares became impossible to obtain from the Eastern Region. Replacement motive power was draughted in from the London Midland which was slowly being dieselised, and electrified in the case of the West Coast main line. The Great Central was relegated to having to use worn-out stock, but rumour had it that the latter situation would only be temporary as the London Extension was to be given the status of a secondary route and dieselised throughout. This plan was short-lived apart from a brief attempt to implement it in 1965. Indeed, the only real evidence of modern traction came at Woodford Halse depot which was extended to provide a small fuelling complex for four 350bhp Diesel Shunters. Leicester and Neasden were also supplied with one and four shunters respectively, but it was Darnall in Sheffield that shedded the majority of modern traction catering for the cross-country and excursion trains using the Great Central. One long distance diesel working originated from Marylebone in the form of a Multiple Unit responsible for the 8.38 am semi-fast diagram to Nottingham Victoria returning at 12.25 pm. Despite the latter, it became clearer as time went on that the Midland Region was eager to press ahead with electrification of the West Coast main line and improve services on the Midland main line from St Pancras to Sheffield, leaving the Great Central to stagnate and decay while its traffic was drained away onto the newly opened M1 motorway which cheekily ran for nineteen miles in close proximity to the London Extension. Evidence of the Midland's desire to boost its own line at the expense of the Great Central came with the transfer of the two crack expresses *The Master Cutler*, and the *South Yorkshireman* to St Pancras whence the two trains run today, the former being a Pullman service, while the latter is designated an Executive. The *Master Cutler* was always a popular train with a regular clientele running between Marylebone and Sheffield, while the Bradford train, *The South Yorkshireman*, was never well patronised due to its unpopular timetable. Nevertheless it did contribute some revenue to the line's coffers.

Gradually it became apparent that eventual closure could be a serious threat as two important trains in the line's make-up had been removed and the line was beginning to show signs of becoming an official dumping ground for worn-out steam locomotives from other regions made redundant by the rapid dieselisation programme. In the Nottingham area, a separate concern reared its head in the form of subsidence due to the expansion of mine workings in the area, which necessitated the imposition of a speed limit on certain sections of the line which added to the journey times at a period when the Great Central was burdened enough. Eventually the shortage of engines which ensued became so acute that some of the high performance 9F class were draughted to the London Extension: a novel experience for the drivers, who enjoyed their efficiency and speed. With this new breed it was possible to improve the timings over the southern section, thus making the speed restrictions in Nottinghamshire less of a drawback. Although the 9Fs had brought a welcome breath of fresh air to the Great Central, the atmosphere was soured by the astonishing decision to axe all the daytime Marylebone to Manchester expresses replacing them with a series of three semi-fast trains in each direction that only went as far as Nottingham, calling sometimes at seven, eight, or even nine stations en route. The trains were formed of six coach rakes with no refreshment cars and all were routed over the Aylesbury section, causing High Wycombe to lose its through Great Central service. This new arrangement was a poor substitute and only served to discourage any potential revenue, as few travellers were likely to be encouraged to travel by a journey time of three hours between London and Nottingham. During the night, however, the pattern of trains remained the same, with the shipment of mail and newspapers to their various destinations. Also unaffected by this decision were the cross-country, local and freight workings.

Up until 1962, the measures adopted were not so dire that they could not be reversed and the line revert to its original status. Complete closure was a different matter, being first proposed in 1962 amidst great concern and protests. Such a measure was unthinkable for the Great Central, but it became a real threat when, instead of the abolition in one complete move, closures were implemented on a piecemeal basis, starting in the summer of 1962 with Neasden Locomotive Depot having its role usurped by Leicester and Annesley. The second part of the closure plan was implemented with great speed the following year. On 4 March 1963 local stations, with some exceptions, were removed from the network. Local services were deemed to be the biggest causes for the heavy losses reported on the London Extension and after an intense investigation into the passenger loadings on trains between Aylesbury and Rugby Central, Woodford and Banbury, and Nottingham and Sheffield, the case had been sealed so far as Dr Beeching (Chairman, British Rail) was concerned. For the locals, replacement bus services were organised but these were considered inconvenient and did not have the added advantage of connecting with the long-distance workings on the railway as the local trains did. In this respect the railway missed out in two ways, losing its local revenue as well as, for example, the long-distance passenger who boarded his train at one of the following stations to go to Sheffield. Those stations involved in the closure to passenger traffic were Quainton, Calvert, Finmere, Helmdon and Charwelton on the Aylesbury to Rugby Central section (Braunston, Willoughby and Culworth being closed to all traffic on 1 April 1957 and 29 September 1958). With regard to the Woodford to Banbury section, although its intermediate stations at Chacombe Road and Eydon Road were closed in 1956, it won a temporary reprieve and finally ceased in 1964. On the section from Rugby to Nottingham Victoria, the stations at Whetstone, Belgrave and Birstall, Rothley,

Quorn and Woodhouse, Rushcliffe Halt, Ruddington and Nottingham Arkwright Street were affected. North of Nottingham Victoria to the end of the London Extension at Annesley Junction, the withdrawal of local trains isolated the communities at Bulwell, Hucknall and Annesley.

In the last years, only Brackley Central, Woodford Halse, Rugby Central, Lutterworth Ashby Magna, Leicester Central, Loughborough Central, East Leake and New Basford, and Nottingham Victoria remained as revenue-earning stations although the 'locals' did continue to handle freight for a short while after their demise. During this period, while the West Coast main line electrification was being carried out between Euston and Manchester, the Great Central was party to a sudden upsurge in traffic, such as the 'Starlight Specials' which were diverted via Bletchley over the Oxford and Cambridge line to Calvert, where they joined the line down into Marylebone.

The Great Central was renowned for its fast and efficient freight services borne out by their nicknames 'Runners' and 'Windcutters' which were bestowed upon them because they were incomparably better than those provided on other regions. The nearest equivalent was the 'Condor' fitted freight trains. These trains mainly carried coal, iron and steel. In addition, the line did a brusque trade conveying fish and parcels and domestic goods. After many years of having the monopoly on freight transportation, these services fell prey to the ever-growing motor-lorry fleets. The removal of freight services was eventually proposed for June 1965 with some 720 wagons per day being diverted to the Birmingham-Barnt Green-Bristol, or Banbury to London routes. Instead of Woodford and Annesley yards catering for the traffic flow, Toton yard was to handle all the traffic, and that which it did not process was eliminated by more block worked trains. So on 14/15 June 1965 disaster struck for one particular town: Woodford Halse, which relied heavily on the railway to provide its inhabitants with employment. To the residents of the town it was unthinkable that freight services could ever be withdrawn, and unbelievable that the complex once described as the 'pride of Europe' with its depot, sheds, marshalling yards, station, goods yard, and junction to four destinations, was to become just another place on the map. The decision to close the complex forever, leaving just the station and a couple of passing loops, forced people to move away and seek employment elsewhere, leaving Woodford Halse to become a ghost town as its skilled workers drifted away. The skeletal passenger service, which served Woodford and the other remaining stations on the route, lingered on until 1966 when, in the early hours of 4 September, the Great Central ceased to be a trunk line. On the previous afternoon, no official send-off took place except for the strenghthening of normal trains and an enthusiasts' special being hauled from Waterloo to Sheffield and back. Thousands turned out to witness the passing of a railway, cut down in the prime of its life after just 67 years of service. From then on, services were run by Diesel Multiple Units between Marylebone and Aylesbury, Marylebone and Banbury, and Rugby Central and Nottingham Arkwright Street which was re-opened on 4 September 1967 when Nottingham Victoria was finally abandoned and handed over for redevelopment. However, the commuter service between Rugby and Nottingham did not last. A deliberate attempt was made to discourage passengers from using the last vestiges of the Great Central by making it impossible to book journeys in advance, running trains at awkward times and, in addition, the staff did not always collect the fares, with the result that on 3 May 1969 another part of the London Extension ceased to exist.

Persecuted on the grounds of being an uneconomic folly, the last stretch of the Great Central empire, Marylebone, was destined to close although at the present time the station has been reprieved, mainly due to improved usage and activity at weekends from the Sunday Luncheon Steam trains to Stratford-upon-Avon and back. Another factor in its favour was the increase in patronage on the Metropolitan trains into Baker Street, which would have had to cope with the extra traffic, along with Paddington, had the station at Marylebone been closed. During the bleak period when closure loomed threateningly over Marylebone, various schemes were put forward for its subsequent use, such as a bus station for National Express, together with a dedicated busway through Lords and West Hampstead tunnels. Even though closure has been mooted there is little doubt that Marylebone will disappear along with the rest of the London Extension. Already the offices of the old Great Central at 222 Marylebone Road have been sold off for conversion back to a hotel, while the station itself is to witness a reduction in the number of platforms and some development on the platform concourse. Supposition is that in the future the Aylesbury service will still use Marylebone, while the High Wycombe to Banbury trains will be worked into and out of Paddington. Other improvements include the introduction of new rolling stock to replace the life-expired units working the line at present, some of which saw main-line service on the London Extension between Marylebone and Nottingham twenty or so years ago.

The Great Central, although closed, has not lost its identity completely, since its trackbed and bridges, and the occasional tunnel, still stand as a reminder to those who built it, worked it and managed the companies who controlled it. Hopefully the collection of more modern plates and the Newton photographs will have shown what a splendid engineering feat the whole line was. Evidence of the latter is apparent from walking the trackbed, as certain features of the line still stand, and it is possible to locate the route through Buckinghamshire, Northamptonshire, Leicestershire, and Nottinghamshire. In the city areas of Leicester and Nottingham the route has more or less been obliterated by the march of time but the age of inter-city steam travel along the Great Central is far from dead between these two places. Efforts are currently in hand to preserve the section of line from Ruddington, just south of Nottingham, to Belgrave and Birstall, just north of Leicester.

The story began back in 1969 when a group of railway enthusiasts in Leicester decided to form an association known as the Main Line Preservation Group with the aim of acquiring a stretch of the former main line and running large steam locomotives on it. Their action was largely prompted by the proposed withdrawal of passenger services on the line between Rugby Central and Nottingham Arkwright Street. It was eventually decided that the most interesting section to purchase would be that between Leicester Abbey Lane and Loughborough Central, although some had had their sights set on Nottingham for the northern terminus.

By 1971, the Main Line Preservation Group was reformed as a charitable trust, which became known as the Main Line Steam Trust who engaged in the task of raising funds and seeking new members at the same time as leasing parts of Loughborough Central station. By 1972 the buildings at Loughborough Central station began to witness a rejuvenation and the first rolling stock and locomotives were soon to arrive on this budding railway. Operations did not begin until 1973, when steam-train rides were offered within the confines of the station complex. Due to the tremendous efforts put in by volunteers and the success of fund-raising, services were able to begin between Loughborough Central and Quorn and Woodhouse in the same year, on 30 September. Some months earlier, on 24 June 1973, the first train run by the Trust on this section had been in the form of a Lobster Bake special to herald the progress made by the volunteers. A temporary setback was suffered though when the British Railways' supervised services were suspended and not recommenced until July 1974. However, the Main Line Steam Trust was subjected to having to pay for the track on a monthly basis while efforts were undertaken to raise sufficient funds for purchase. Meanwhile services were extended to Rothley on 6 September 1975.

By 1976 the Main Line Steam Trust were faced with the dilemma of having to pay for the track or see it lifted and witness the passing of the dream of a handful of enthusiasts. The Trust then organised the formation of a public limited company and the launching of a share issue, which was successful in that it secured the purchase of the single line between Loughborough and Rothley. The double-track option was no longer viable and British Rail lifted this second track along with both lines to Belgrave and Birstall.

The trackbed to Belgrave and Birstall was subsequently purchased and leased back to the railway by Charnwood Borough Council to allow for the eventual extension of the line, which is currently under way. This will bring the total distance to 8½ miles through some of the finest Leicestershire countryside, through the Charnwood Hills and over Swithland Reservoir. In addition to the expansion to Belgrave and Birstall, work is now in hand to secure the section of line from Ruddington to Rushcliffe Halt, which will form part of the northern extension. The second stage of this project will incorporate the portion between Rushcliffe and Loughborough which is currently in use by British Rail for gypsum trains. One of the problems with this project is the need to fill in the gap left by the removal of the original embankment and establish a bridge over the Midland main line to Nottingham and London. Once the embankment is rebuilt and a new bridge installed north of Loughborough Central, it will once again be possible to enjoy the delights of travelling by steam train between Leicester and Nottingham.